How To Turn Off Your Brain
And Listen To God

THE
GREATEST
TRUTH
IN THE
UNIVERSE

TARRENT-'AUTHUR' HENRY

Absolute Author
Publishing House

Copyright © 2023 Tarrent-'Authur' Henry

ISBN 978-1-64953-828-4 (paperback)
ISBN 978-1-64953-829-1 (ebook)

All rights reserved. No part of this book may be reproduced, stored, or transmitted by any means—whether auditory, graphic, mechanical, or electronic—without written permission of the author, except in the case of brief excerpts used in critical articles and reviews. Unauthorized reproduction of any part of this work is illegal and is punishable by law.

CONTENTS

Acknowledgements..5
Introduction..7
Chapter 1: "Two Questions" 9
Chapter 2: "Margaret" 21
Chapter 3: "Public Saxophone"..33
Chapter 4: "The Trapezoid" 47
Chapter 5: "Moses Aaron" 60
Chapter 6: "Desdemona" 73
Chapter 7: "Community" 86
Chapter 8: "RSL" 94
Chapter 9: "Flight" 109
Chapter 10: "Turn Off Your Brain" 122
Conclusion...137
About The Author..139

ACKNOWLEDGEMENTS

I would be remiss if I didn't first thank God the Father, God the Son and God the Holy Spirit for saving me, keeping me, and pouring into me the words contained on these pages that you are about to digest. Lord, I am nothing without You.

My amazing bride, Helen for loving me unconditionally and being my better half. For being in my corner and giving me the time, space and understanding as I partook in writing this manuscript. And for being a gifted writer, having written three books to date. "Telling it All from the Heart", "Women on the R.U.N. for Jesus" and "Transforming Lives -A Three Step Guide in Becoming a Better You." Helen, you mean more to me than words could ever say. Sweetness, I love you so!

Miguel and Ed, my two sensational step-sons. I pray this blessing over your lives: that you will always honor God, love your wives and provide for your children. I pray for Godly wisdom, guidance, and direction. I pray for health, wealth, and long lives. I pray that you will be the head and not the tail, above and not beneath and that you will leave a legacy for your children's children. Love you, guys!

And to all the other people who have managed to wiggle in and out of my life over the past umpteen years. Know that I love and appreciate you and I pray that you've found what you were looking for.

INTRODUCTION

I don't really remember all the details but when I rose while lying on the bed, I took my last breath. But I sensed in the spirit that it wasn't my time. *(satan has been trying to kill me and will continue to try to trick and deceive me)* I called on the name of Jesus and from deep in my heart, quickly and instantly, satan's hand was taken from around my throat. *(the hand that was seeking to choke the life out of me)* And I could take a deep spiritual breath. Then the Lord began to deal with me about the state-of-my-heart and with my walk with Him. I vow never to get that far from God again. (Monday August 11th, 2003)

There is no magic formula to establish a right relationship with God except His Word. And in order to establish a secure relationship with our Lord and Savior, the Word must produce your thinking; your thinking produce your emotions; your emotions produce your decisions; your decisions produce your actions; your actions produce your habits; your habits produce your character and your character produce your destiny. This formula will help determine how your life will end up. Brothers and sisters, we must stop looking to and at the world for our destiny. Our destiny starts with **Kingdom Thinking** and ends with **Kingdom Building**. We must learn to look to God for our healing, wealth, happiness, peace, and any need that lines up with **HIS WORD.** *For no matter how many promises God has made, they are "Yes" in Christ. And so through him the "Amen" is spoken by us to the glory of God. (2 Corinthians 1:20 – NIV)* God, has a plan saints. And it starts with **YOU** and ends with **YOU!**

Let us pray:

> *"Father, help me invest my life in people who will grow strong and who will bring forth good fruit! I want to give my life to people who are going to do something in this world. I want to know that I have made a difference in the life of someone who is going to make a difference in the lives of others. The last thing I want is to have lived this life without ever making a personal investment in anyone else, so please help me recognize those people You want me to pour myself into. Then give me the wisdom and grace to pull up alongside and share with them the treasure You have placed in me!" In Jesus name, I pray.*

My challenge is to you, my brothers and sisters. My challenge is to the believer and the unbeliever. The New Christian and the Old Christian. To the leaders in the church and to those that take up a pew. It's time to **"TURN OFF YOUR BRAIN AND LISTEN TO GOD……..**

Chapter One

"TWO QUESTIONS"

*"Do you remember what your life was like
before the storm cloud flooded every situation?
How everything came so easy to you?
Well I am alive and living today,
living proof that miracles do occur.
As the world turns more violent each day
as prices go up and values come down.
I choose to turn to God."*
(Tarrent-Authur Henry)

I would like to ask you two questions? If you were to die tonight, where would you go? The second question I would like to ask, are you sure?

You were planned for God's pleasure. You were formed for God's family. You were created to become like Christ. You were shaped for serving God. You were made for a mission.

Please Pray this Aloud with me: *Lord Jesus, I believe that you are God. I believe that you went to the cross to die for me. I believe that you rose from the dead. Lord Jesus, I am a sinner and I want to repent of my sin right now. Lord Jesus, come into my heart and take control of my life. Right now, Jesus, Right now! In your precious name, I pray, Amen.*

If you prayed that prayer already, congratulations, you are family. If you prayed that prayer for the first time, welcome to God's family. There are four things I need you to do:

1. Join a church where the Bible is taught.
2. Receive Water Baptism by Immersion.
3. Acquire and learn to read your Bible daily.
4. Learn how to pray in the name of Jesus.

There are three responsibilities you need to become Christ like:

1. Let go of your old lifestyle.
2. Change the way you think. (Let the Holy spirit transform your mind)
3. Develop new Godly habits.

As you read your Bible and begin to observe, interpret, and apply God's Word to every situation in your life, an amazing transformation will take place. You will find yourself becoming a different kind of person. Old habits will be dropped, and new Godly ones developed. You will be changed. You will be hooked. You will be excited.

God uses His Word, people, and circumstances to mold us. God's Word provides the truth that we need to grow. God's people provide the support we need to flow. God's circumstances provide the environment we need to practice Christlikeness. For a man/woman is a slave to whatever has mastered them. You once majored in the world; it's time to major in Christ.

Father God sent His Son Jesus into the world so that through Him (Jesus) the world might be saved. *(John 3:17)* Jesus, the Son of God was manifested to destroy the works of (satan) the devil. *(1 John 3:8)* Jesus hung, bled, and died on a tree at Calvary, to save a wretch like you and like me.

Let us go to the Word of God in the Book of Luke*: Then one of the criminals who were hanged blasphemed Him, saying, "If You are the Christ, save Yourself and us. But the other, answering, rebuked him, saying, "Do you not even fear God, seeing you are under the same con-*

demnation? And we indeed justly, for we receive the due reward of our deeds; but this Man has done nothing wrong." Then he said to Jesus, "Lord, remember me when You come into Your kingdom." And Jesus said to him, "Assuredly, I say to you, today you will be with Me in Paradise." (Luke 23:39-43 – NKJV)

Holy scriptures identifies these men as thieves who were crucified with Jesus, one on the right and one on the left side of Him. The sinner on the left is identified as the impenitent (bad) thief and the sinner on the right the penitent (good) thief. The thief on the left was named Gestas (complain, moan) and the thief on the right was named Dismas (sunset, death). The Bible teaches us that Gestas spoke negative, degrading words toward Jesus denying his Deity but Dismas corrected Gestas while at the same time acknowledging that they were both sinners, guilty and deserved the penalty of death due them and realized who it was that was next to him and asked the Lord to forgive Him and remember him. And Jesus said, (paraphrase mine) Amen, I say to you, you are already with Me in My Kingdom.

I ask you if you were to die tonight where would you go? Are you impenitent or penitent? Are you a Gestas or a Dismas? Tomorrow is not promised to you. The question is for tonight and not tomorrow because no one really knows the day and time *(Matthew 24:36)* only the Father knows. God's Will is for you to be in His Kingdom.

> *As for him who lacks understanding, [God's] Wisdom says to him, Come, eat of my bread and drink of the [spiritual] wine which I have mixed. (Proverbs 9:4b-5 - AMPC)*

This happened right after a church service......One of the deacons made an announcement: "Any brother or sister interested in providing safe transport for Sister Margaret will you please meet us in the back of the sanctuary?" Now when Brother Dennis heard the deacon's announcement, he got really scared. You see, Brother Dennis lived on the same block and in the same building that Sister Margaret did. Brother Dennis, slipped out the side door of the church, hustled his family into his car and sped off. Three days later, Brother Dennis

got a speeding ticket while he was on his way home from work. As Brother Dennis waited for the police officer to issue the citation. The Holy Spirit spoke to Brother Dennis. Brother Dennis was issued the summons and proceeded to drive home. He parked his Volkswagen Rabbit and said, "Holy Spirit, how was I supposed to fit a big 350-pound woman in my car?" Nevertheless, Brother Dennis was convicted as he entered the building and punched the elevator button for the third floor; he lived on the fifth. A knock-on Apartment 3G brought a "Praise the Lord, who is it?" "Brother Dennis, Sister Margaret." Sister Margaret came out of her favorite room, the kitchen and opened the door. "Can we talk, ma'am?" Sister Margaret let him in. Brother Dennis slowly started to blurt out his confession. Sister Margaret, went into the kitchen and lowered the fire from under the pot of greens which was on the stove; then she said, "No offense, Brother Dennis but you drive too fast!" "Brother Dennis, I'd rather walk than ride in your car!" Then Sister Margaret started to laugh; Brother Billy took me home in his Escalade!" Then Brother Dennis started to laugh! "Sister Margaret, this isn't a speeding ticket; it's a disobedience ticket!" "God was trying to warn me through you Sister Margaret, that I was sinning by driving my car too fast and I missed it...
What are you running from; what are you missing, fool?

> *Now therefore listen to me, O you sons; for blessed (happy, fortunate, to be envied) are those who keep my ways. Hear instruction and be wise, and do not refuse or neglect it. Blessed (happy, fortunate, to be envied) is the man who listens to me, watching daily at my gates, waiting at the posts of my doors. For whoever finds me [Wisdom] finds life and draws forth and obtains favor from the Lord. But he who misses me or sins against me wrongs and injures himself; all who hate me love and court death. (Proverbs 8:32-36 - AMPC)*

God has a plan, brothers and sisters. And it starts with – **YOU** – it ends with **YOU**. Now here are the steps we need to take, if we are to develop a strong Christian relationship:

1. Get rid of thoughts contrary to God's Word and Will.
2. Always be prepared to give your testimony.
3. You are the "The Body of Christ".
4. Sit under anointed Leadership.
5. Total commitment always through trials and triumphs is required.
6. You are either in Christ or for the devil.
7. Be in full partnership with Jesus.
8. Don't forsake your (**B**eliever's **I**nstruction **B**efore **L**eaving **E**arth) Bible.
9. Make Praise and Worship a lifestyle.
10. Develop a Prayer life.

God selected and elected you before he spoke the world into existence. I don't know about you but when I found out that God already knew me that excited me! When I found out that some big-bang theory did not create me, that I was not some accident. There is not one single human being on earth that is a surprise to God. When I knew, I was a child of the King; I had to walk worthy of my High Calling. I said, "Yes", to Christ and my past became just that. I could rejoice again! Right where you are is where God wants to use you; if you been abused, God's got you. In an addiction, He's there for you. God is an ever-present help in time of trouble. *(Psalm 46:1)* Doctor devil gave you a bad report; Doctor Jesus says," by His stripes you are healed". *(Isaiah 53:5)* Brothers and sisters, you didn't choose God; God chose you!

It's time to stop living a life of independence and let's face it where has it gotten you? Choose today to live a life of interdependence; choose it by saying, Lord Jesus, I need you to take control of my life. Some of us have been blinded for years but you can choose today to be free. Receive Salvation (deliverance from sin and its consequences) and Sanctification (being made Holy) and being

Consecrated (dedicated to God's service). It's time to choose to live the Blessed Life, the God-kind-of-life. Choose today what kind of life you'd rather live. *(Joshua 24:15)*

> *Now I saw a new heaven and a new earth, for the first heaven and the first earth had passed away. Also there was no more sea. Then I, saw the holy city, New Jerusalem, coming down out of heaven from God, prepared as a bride adorned for her husband. And I heard a loud voice from heaven saying, "Behold, the tabernacle of God is with men, and He will dwell with them, and they shall be His people. God Himself will be with them and be their God. And God will wipe away every tear from their eyes; there shall be no more death, nor sorrow, nor crying. There shall be no more pain, for the former things have passed away." Then He who sat on the throne said, "Behold, I make all things new." And He said to me, "Write: (Revelation 21:1-5 - NKJV)*

What could be farther from the truth? *"If God is for us, who can be against us?" (Romans 8:31)* I was in a dark place. Have you ever been in a dark place? I was alone. I was very cold and scared. Not wanting to live but not ready to die. Life can be so cruel, sometimes. I was desperate, desperate for a miracle. Then I had this vision and I saw my future wife, funny, because I hadn't even met her yet. She was beautiful and more alluring than any woman I could have imagined or deserved for that matter. Dressed in white and a veil covered her face and her hair flowed and when she moved my stomach started to quiver. My body began to shake uncontrollably, and tears began to flow from my eyes, and I felt a presence, a feeling I had never felt before. Was this love or was this God?

There comes a time in your life when what you dream becomes reality. Your dream becomes so real you can taste it, an *"ice cream dream"*. My favorite flavor is chocolate. What's yours?

I remember this song by Anna B. Warner that we use to sing in Sunday School at the Red Hook Gospel Assembly in Brooklyn, New York. Our Pastor was Reverend Hopkins. He, his wife, and children served the Lord faithfully and taught me about Jesus' love for me:

Jesus loves me! This I know,
For the Bible tells me so;
Little ones to Him belong;
They are weak, but He is strong.

Refrain: Yes, Jesus loves me!
Yes, Jesus loves me! Yes, Jesus loves me!
The Bible tells me so.

Jesus loves me! This I know,
As He loved so long ago,
Taking children on His knee,
Saying, "Let them come to Me."

Jesus loves me still today,
Walking with me on my way,
Wanting as a friend to give
Light and love to all who live.

Jesus loves me! He who died
Heaven's gate to open wide;
He will wash away my sin,
Let His little child come in.

Jesus loves me! He will stay
Close beside me all the way;
Thou hast bled and died for me,
I will henceforth live for Thee.

You may have picked up this book accidently but know that it wasn't by accident it was by *"divine appointment"* that you happened to open this book and started to read. Keep reading my friend, you are about to become experienced? Experienced in what you might ask? Read on:

"Let me tell you about the city of my birth, where I learned to swear and curse. The home of White Rock and TayLord Jeans. The Discotheque named the Club Serene. Any guesses? The answer is Brooklyn, S-C-R-E-A-M IT OUT!!! If you're from B-K, S-H-O-U-T IT OUT!!!" I am just reminiscing about the summers in my home town back in the '70's. AM Radio was big in those days. WWRL – "SUPER 16" with Gregory, Gerry B, Bobby J, Hank Spann, Jeffrey Troy and Garry Byrd with the "GBE". Frankie Crocker was launching WLIB-FM which later became WBLS – "World's Best Looking Sound" with Ken Webb, Vy Higginsen, Lamarr Renee and Captain Midnight Al Roberts.

Youth has its privileges and its virtues and youth is a stage that we all go through. (Yes, Jesus loves me) In school we pledged allegiance to the rag. (opps I mean flag) of the United States of America and to the Republic for Richard Spam (opps…which it stands) one nation under God, invisible (opps…indivisible) for liberty and justice for Robert Hall (opps…all). Youth also has its folly as I learned on many occasions. I became quite familiar with the principal's office.

Super Heros especially Marvel Super Heros: Captain America, Hulk, Iron Man, Thor, Spider Man and Daredevil – "The Man Without Fear". The Avengers, Fantastic Four and the X-men.

Depending on the season, playing baseball, basketball, and football. Learning how to be part of a team. The Drum and Bugle Corp and the Cub Scouts. Learning Discipline. These are all things I experienced growing up in my home town.

When did you lose your innocence? When did you realize that you were not quite like the others? When did fantasy become reality to you? When did life finally sink in?

I woke up this morning and I looked around, I couldn't laugh, I could only frown. A bee was buzzing round my head, I knew if he stung me I'd be dead.

Bee hovered in the air and looked at me, You could have caught me but you set me free. That honey bee had remembered my face, He flapped his wings and buzzed into space.

Then I heard a hissing on the ground, I turned my head and began to look down. Snake was slithering onto the bed, I knew if she bite me I'd be dead.

Snake picked up her head and looked at me, You could have trapped me but you let me be. That snake had remembered my kind act, She cuddled beside me and coiled in my lap.

A familiar sound pierced the air, My body was suddenly filled with fear. Mother was coming her feet being led, I knew if she saw me I'd be dead.

Mother threw the covers off the bed and looked at me, Do I look like a snake or a honey bee? God gave you dominion over the bee, snake and giraffe, But you have no authority over a mother's wrath.

    Poetry helped me to lose my innocence. It showed me that I possessed a special talent that was not like anyone else I knew. Vocabulary expression turned my fantasy into reality and life finally began to sink in and make sense.

    There are many people who are walking around today with no sense of direction or purpose. Sure, they get up every morning, but they are just going through the motions of life. Some may even seem like they are the life of the party but sadly they always go home alone to a house that will never really be their home. I know, I was once one of them.

    You try to use escapism to hide the tears that you cry late at night when you are alone. You wish the phone would ring as you are dying to talk to anyone. Why won't somebody call or knock at my door?

People look and stare at you like you are from another planet. No matter how hard you try, you just don't seem to fit in with the crowd.

You are probably asking yourself; Authur where are you going with this? Right now, I'm just trying to put words together to make a sentence and if I put enough words together, I would have made a paragraph and if I write enough paragraphs, I might have enough pages for a book. Do you catch where I am going with this?

For as far as the naked eye can see, remember reader you will always have me. Conscience *is an inner feeling or voice viewed as acting as a guide to the rightness or wrongness of one's behavior.* Now that's deep. Did you know that sometimes your only friend, talks, looks, and feels like you and you do the same as them? In our quest, our search for companionship, a common phrase used, is a dog is a *"person's best friend."* Did I hear somebody say, *"a canine can't be mine!"* Or maybe that was my conscience speaking to me from my past, recalling *"Where was you at"* by War the Music Band?

Have you ever found yourself walking down the street like the homeless woman in the song, *"Gypsy Woman" by Crystal Waters saying "ladadeeladeeda"*? Can I share a statistic with you? One out of five adults in the U.S., experience serious mental illness and since there are not enough metal illness treatment centers to diagnosis and treat all these people, they are walking among us like the dead walking amongst the living. I know, I was one of them.

If you are one of the fortunate to have been diagnosed and treated for a mental illness you may have been introduced to some form of psychotherapy or prescribed various medications or maybe you were a part of a 12-step program or encouraged to join a support group. There are many complementary and alternative treatments. This book is going to focus on the one I found and hope you will too, to be the most excellent one.

Mr. Jones went to see a psychiatrist and as he sat in the chair the psychiatrist asked Mr. Jones, "What brings you to my office today"? "Doc, I think that I am a dog", he said. The Doctor replied, "How long have you had this problem"? Mr. Jones quickly said, "Ever since I was a puppy!"

I chose this little humorous fictional story to shed a little light on our subject. And in the subsequent chapters I am going to be sharing some actual stories and life events about real people though their names have been changed to protect their anonymity.

I am going to take you on several adventures, and I believe that by the time you finished reading and digesting the information on each page of this one-of-a-kind book that you will look at yourself through a lens that you have never seen through before. I GUARANTEE that you will need to read this book over and over again.

> *When life throws you a curve ball and you swing, and miss, Remember, it's only strike two. When you fumble the football There is always time to recover, Remember, it's only second down. When you take the last second shot and totally miss the basket, Remember, It's only half-time.*
>
> *Remember, life is just a game that we play. Life is just a situated comedy. And Life is a dance, that sometimes leads to romance. No, life is a poem, that says, keep being strong.*

Now let's get back to those two questions:

If you were to die tonight, where would you go? The second question I would like to ask, are you sure?

Many of us remember this prayer taught to us to say when we were children before went to sleep:

> *Now I lay me down to sleep,*
> *I pray the Lord my Soul to keep;*
> *If I should die before I 'wake,*
> *I pray the Lord my Soul to take.*

But do any of us really know? If you were to die tonight? Where would you go?

Can I share something with you? Reader, you may be already dead?

You may already be tired of living your ordinary mundane life?
You may have already thrown in the towel?
You may be so tired of COVID, POLITICS and MOBY DICK?
You may be slowly sinking in quicksand?
You may already be losing money on Bitcoin?
You may be tired of waiting for your ship you never sent out, to come in?
You may never be the next Marvel Superhero?
Or Host of Jeopardy?
Next Oprah Winfrey?
But as John C. Maxwell says: *"The greatest mistake we make is living in constant fear that we will make one."*

This book is going to show you how to stop living in fear and how to live by faith. Faith in what you know not what you tend to believe. Faith in the Creator of the Universe. Faith in yourself. Faith in others who see your dream and as John C. Maxwell teaches: *"Teamwork makes the dream work."*

It's time for you to purpose to know, that you know, that you know. Where are you going and whose side you are on? It's time to get down to the real nitty gritty. It's time to turn the page and start to read Chapter Two.

Chapter Two

"MARGARET"
(Child of light; pearl; jewel)

Margaret or as her family and friends call her Peggy was born in a quaint quiet village in Smalltown, U.S.A. She was born with red hair and green eyes a combination that is considered rare as well as yellowish teeth which is not so rare. She is of average height with an average build and is of above average intelligence. Let's follow along as she tells her story:

I don't know where to start. As a child growing up, I always thought I was different. I had the rare distinction of being a green-eyed red-headed "Geekgirl." I always wanted to be in pictures. Two of my idols are Drew Barrymore and Lindsay Lohan not only because they are drop-dead gorgeous but because we share the same rarity. Little did I know that in time that would not be the only thing we had in common.

> *If by chance, I ever be a star,*
> *I'll remember you though I may be far,*
> *All that fame and glory be,*
> *remember lover you will always have me.*
> *You were with me when times were hard.*
> *And when I felt insecure*
> *you stood by me like a guard.*

My mother said, I shouldn't let you go,
But instead of listening to my mother.
I powered my nose with snow. (cocaine)

Yeah, when I went to Hollywood, I went from "Geekgirl" to "SnowQueen." Instead of starring in action films I was starring in private movies. I became:

Champagne Ann – super star
Hottest young thing in this bar
Champagne Ann – super star
I'm your super star baby!

I was being served for breakfast, lunch, and dinner. I was so twisted I started answering and calling myself Champagne Annie. I was the life of the party, making all kinds of money doing things that nice little red-haired green-eyed "Geekgirls" shouldn't do. I was one, "hot-mess."

I was just a child (17) trying to be a grown-up woman in a city that was known to chew up and spit out small-town girls like me. Before I knew it I had a pimp calling all the shots for me. I couldn't go, do, or say anything without his permission. He even forbade me to contact my family. I didn't know it then but I was soon being trafficked for sex.

The devil has got a hold of me
and I want to go home.
I don't need to be here; don't want to be here.
Don't want to live anymore.
Just want to die.
I can't take the abuse anymore.
The beatings. The drugs.
How did I end up here?
Can somebody hear me?
Will somebody help me?
Please, Lord............
Give me a second chance?

Then the worst thing that could have happened to me happened. I got arrested. But sometimes what looks bad at first turns out to be a good thing. I was riding in the car with my pimp going to a party when we suddenly got pulled over. Scared for his sorry ass, he made me put the drugs he had in his stash in my purse, and you guessed it, I was arrested.

I watched astonishly as he told the officers that he didn't know me and was only giving me a ride and those cops believed every lie as I was searched, handcuffed, and arrested. The cops threw me into the backseat of the patrol car and took me to the station to be booked.

You have the right to remain silent. Anything you say can be used against you in court. You have the right to talk to a lawyer for advice before we ask you any questions. You have the right to have a lawyer with you during questioning. If you cannot afford a lawyer, one will be appointed for you before any questioning if you wish. If you decide to answer questions now without a lawyer present, you have the right to stop answering at any time.

I was read my Miranda rights for the first time and since I was high, scared and confused I wouldn't or couldn't respond. Then like a tornado I felt my stomach erupt and the full contents of my stomach from the 'shrimp lo mein' that I ate earlier came up and unto the arresting officer and the rest spew all over me and immediately I collapsed and felt unto the floor and into my vomit.

> *There is no place like home.*
> *There is no place like home.*
> *I've been to Paris.*
> *I've been to Rome.*
> *But there is no place like home.*

When I woke up, I couldn't move. I had all kinds of different tubes in my body, and I was restrained to the bed. I was so weak. I couldn't speak. I had fake ID on me so there was no one to contact. Since I had never been arrested or had my fingerprints taken, I was not in the system, so I technically didn't exist. I laid in that hospital bed in ICU, moving in and out of a coma for three weeks until I slowly began to recover.

The doctors, nurses and staff began to remove some of the tubes that seem to be coming from everywhere on my body. I was weak and barely able to speak. When they asked me my name, I was shocked when I said Peggy.

An olive-skinned nurse was one of the first people I spoke with after I regained full consciousness. Her voice was so distinctive, and I remember telling her that I heard her voice someplace before. She told me her name was Angel and she had been praying for me every day for the last several weeks. After she spoke those words to me, I never saw her again.

I was soon transferred to another room. This room was private, but I had a female police officer standing guard outside my door twenty-four- seven while I was in recovery. The officer who worked the 1600-2400 shift from Wednesday to Sunday was not like the other officers. She would pop her head from time to time and ask me how I was doing and when she was able, this officer Gwen would grab a chair and sit down and talk to and with me. She made me feel alive and I felt human again like a woman and not a piece of property.

Gwen was also a Chaplain and with my permission she took the time to minister to my pain. She didn't open the Bible to preach to me rather she open her heart and touched mine. And oh, how I needed to feel my heart again. When Gwen hugged me, I felt like a baby being held by its mother for the first time. She begged me to share my family information with her, but I lied and told her I didn't have any. I was still too ashamed to face them. Gwen not once pressured me but lovingly mothered me back to reality.

Gwen, shared with me her personal story. She told a story of a young, fat, black, ugly child that everyone said wouldn't amount to anything. Officer Taylor was so transparent. She talked about the times when she was raped by family members and the shame it put her through. Her story gave me hope that if Gwen could make it through a difficult period in her life so could I.

Looking at Gwen today, you see a tall, brown, statuesque woman with a heart of gold. Then suddenly, just like Angel. Gwen was replaced on the second shift by another professional cop.

The doctors determined that I could be released from the hospital. I was issued an orange suit that looked like hospital scrubs and told, not asked to put it on while another female cop watched. Then she handcuffed me, much too tight and herded me out of the hospital making sure to take the scenic route so everybody could see I was in her custody. I despised her, under my breath and in my heart.

I soon learned I was heading to central arraignment to be officially charged. I was assigned a legal attorney named Raphael and she advised me on what I was facing. I was being hit with a felony drug charge. My attorney said, *"Peggy, I am asking you to trust me today. You can plead guilty, and the judge will probably put you on probation and let you go free, but you will have a record, but I am asking you to plead not guilty and trust me."* My fictious name was called, *"Ann Redd".* The judge said, *"How does the defendant plead?"* I looked at my attorney and nodded my head as she responded, *"The defendant pleads not guilty!"*

The judge looked in the direction of the arresting officer, *"you have charged the defendant Ann Redd with criminal possession of a controlled substance. Where is the evidence"?* The arresting officer looked at the judge and said, *"Your Honor, we are unable to provide any evidence at this time". "Do you mean to tell me that this woman was detained in the hospital for over three months, and you have no evidence of her having possessed any controlled substance?" "Case closed and the charges dismissed. Ann Redd you are free to leave the Court House pending the signing of the release documents."*

Maybe I was seeing things, but I could have sworn I saw Nurse Angel and Officer Gwen when I turned around to walk out of the courtroom and to freedom.

Raphael was with me every step of the way as we grabbed my things that were taken away from me while I was in police custody, I quickly threw them in the trash and with that, my past. She insisted that I leave with her through the attorney entrance to avoid any contact with anyone I might not want to see. I insisted I would be okay, but Raphael persisted, and I let her help me. She brought me to a place that I would call home for the next six months.

We made our way through the underground garage and hopped into her red BMW Z4 convertible and headed for the Pacific Coast Highway with the wind at my back and sun in my face. It felt like we were *"Thelma and Louise"* without all the drama. I was so relaxed and soaked in all that I had missed while I was being trafficked. What was it now, six years of my life chasing after the wrong dream?

Along the way, we stopped at the mall in Long Beach and Raphael being the sweetheart that she is, charged some new outfits and accessories that I would need for my new place of residence. Then it was back on the road with the music of Tom Petty and the Heartbreakers, *"Free Fallin"* playing as our national anthem.

Raphael broke the silence and took me out of my ethereal trance. *"Peggy, are you hungry?"* Raphael told me that her father wanted a girl, but it turns our Raphael is a gender-neutral name. Her mother is Spanish, and her father Italian and she speaks both fluently. Raphael is tanned, slightly taller than me with dark hair and eyes with a calm, cool, confident demeanor. We soon became fast friends and best buds during our short time together.

We decided to stop to eat in Malibu to enjoy the sights and food. It had been so long since I tasted real food and had a real friend who seemed to value my friendship. Before all I had were wife-in-laws or sister-wives as we were called. It felt good to have a girlfriend that called me by my familiar name, Peggy. Raphael, *"I was meaning to ask you. How did you know my name was Peggy?" "Do you want the long version or the short, Red?"*

She went on the explain how there is a state-by-state list of people that are missing and possible targets of human trafficking. Raphael lost a dear friend to human trafficking that was later killed and since that time she has been a strong advocate for reform. She happened to be going through the list in her office one day and my name just happened to be on that list. *"How many green-eyed, red-heads do you know?"* she said. *"When I was assigned your case, I took a chance I called you Peggy and when you didn't object, I knew I found you. Call it chance or call it God?"*

I look at all the little boys and all the little girls,
And I think to myself who is watching over them?
I look at them and then I look at me,
I'm so thankful that God remembered me.

We finished our meal and headed back to Raphael's red convertible, but it was gone. We searched and searched. High and low we searched but it became obvious that someone had stolen our scarlet chariot.

Raph, was so cool and it kind of, sort of rubbed off on me. She took her iPhone out of her black Gucci purse and notified the insurance company. Geico took her report and promised to have a replacement car at the mall within the hour and filed the police report for her as well. In the meantime, we hit the stores to re-purchase all the items that were stolen with the vehicle.

Soon, we were back on the road in a Honda convertible. We put my new accessories in the trunk. Raphael promised that we would reach our destination by nightfall, but I didn't pay much attention, I was caught up in the moment. Thinking about my family and what I was going to do with my life now that I was free.

I was so glad that I was free. Free from drugs. Free from pimps. Free from johns, Free to redo and relive my life.

When we arrived at our destination. Raph, had to wake me up as I had fallen asleep. *"This is as far as I go"*, she said as she popped open the trunk. *"You can grab your things and walk through that gate, it's your choice?"* I slowly opened the door and walked to the rear of the Honda but before I could reach in to grab my things, I felt the most loving arms you could image take me in and give me the biggest sincerest hug as if she knew what I needed and Raph gave me the biggest kiss as tears flowed from her eyes as we said our last goodbyes and final farewells. Like Angel and Gwen, I knew Raphael was on special assignment and I would never see or hear from her again.

I walked through the gates as Raphael turned the Honda around and sped off into the night. I rang the bell and immediately the door opened, and the gate closed behind me. A tall tan lady with a strong Spanish accent said, *"Bienvenido a refugio Seguro"* which means, Welcome to Safe Haven. She took the bags from my hands and introduced herself as Senora Maria.

I was taken to the reception area where I was warmly greeted by the staff. *"You must be tired from your long journey,"* a woman with a Caribbean accent said. *"Maria, take her to her room and let her get settled in." "Peggy, we will talk in the morning. If you need anything, Maria will provide it for you."* The clock on the wall said 8:30. As soon as my head hit the pillow, I fell into lala land.

The phone rang in my room. Since I haven't heard or had a phone in such a long time, I was initially startled. But I soon recovered and realized that I wasn't dreaming, the phone in my room was actually ringing. *"Hello!" "Good, morning, Peggy, Rise and shine!" "Breakfast, is in an hour, there is a shower in your room and if you need anything just pick up the phone and dial 0."* From the sound of the strong Spanish accent, I knew it was Senora Maria.

After breakfast, it was time for my orientation with the woman with the Caribbean accent. She would become the most important person in my life for the next six months. Her name was Queen Esther Jenkins from the island of Martinique.

First, I had to be deprogrammed. I was isolated from everyone for the first fourteen days that I was there. I only had contact with the staff as they put together a program for my total recovery to assume my identity once again as Margaret "Peggy" Smythe.

Since, I was discharged from the hospital I was no longer taking the medications that they were giving me, as the days went on, my personality began to change. I began to experience extreme highs and would often sink into a deep depression. I would have recurring dreams of my previous life and would often wake up at night screaming and in a cold sweat. But no matter what I was going through there always seem to be a sincere, caring staff member always watching over me.

The staff lived on-site and was well trained and each member had the patience of Job and made me feel like family. Then one morning, I woke up and all the past hurt, pain and anxiety seem to be completely gone. Without drugs, tough love, or isolation, I was starting to feel less like Ann and more like "Peggy".

"*Today,* Queen Esther spoke with her soothing voice, *you are going to meet the rest of the family, Peggy.*" I was never more excited as I was introduced to the other five female residents that would become my family for the next 168 days.

I was reintroduced to tennis and played it for the first time in years, though rusty I still had a powerful serve. The art therapy relaxed me, and I was even introduced and started to take on-line courses to complete my GED and enroll in college. My life was slowly starting to come back into focus.

Two months and then three months passed, I watched my life take a 180-degree turnaround. Though chapel and bible study were made available they were not a requirement but most of us participated freely and willingly including the Muslim girl that found herself being sex trafficked from Pakistan. Alisha, as her name means, was now being protected by God. She was trying to learn English and she and I soon became best buds.

During, my fourth month, it came time for Alisha to leave. Since she had no known family in the U.S.A. and nowhere to go, she was able to enroll in college to continue her studies. Queen Esther managed to arrange for a family to take her in and provide for her as she continued her recovery from all the trauma that she experienced being taken from her home country and trafficked all over the world. We promised to stay in touch and connect after my stay was up.

I was never pressured to contact my family but after my fifth month I suddenly had the urge to call my mother. It was Mother's Day and I suddenly realized how much I missed her. My ability to feel empathy was starting to come back as Doctor Brown predicted. He said, *"It will hit you like a lightning strike, one day!"*

I was so nervous. I picked up the phone and began to dial. I started to hang up, just as the phone rang. But before I could disconnect, I heard the bestest, sweetest voice in the whole universe, the only voice sweeter to your ear than Jesus, the voice that you'll remember even after the day you die. That voice for me was, Elizabeth Blair Smythe. *"H-e-l—lo",* she sang. I paused before I said, *"Mama!"*

It seemed like an eternity before I heard her next word. *"Paapaa, Peggy, is that you!" "Is that you, Meggy Peggy?" "Mama, Mama, oh how I missed you Mama,"* as tears streamed from my eyes and down my face. There was a brief silence as mama's pent-up tears began to fall too. What had it been six, seven years since she heard her Meggy Peggy's voice?

Before I got off the phone with her, I spoke to Papa. Drew, my baby brother. Big Sis, Belinda and Aunt Claire and Uncle Buck, talk about tears, we cried us an ocean. I made plans to come home to see them after my time was up here at *"Bienvenido a refugio Seguro"*

Time was moving quickly with all the folks coming and leaving. Queen Esther said that 98% of the people that leave, live a brand-new life, free from the past life that had them bound. One night, Queen Esther decided to share her story with me, and I was cut to shreds that she was ever able to survive all that she went through. She said, *"it was by the grace of God that she didn't die."* A nine-year-old anybody, should not have had to go through what she did, but she survived to live to tell her story and open up a place to help others who had undergone a similar plight. Thank God for Queen Esther Jenkins'.

July, came and went and so did I. My day of redemption had come. My six-month stay was over. They threw a farewell party for me as they do for all the former residents. We cried happy tears together knowing that we may never see each other again but knowing that we can go out and face the world again. We might have fallen down big time, but we got up bigger, better, stronger and wiser.

I lost touch with Alisha. While staying with her host family she was able to connect with some relatives who lived in New York, so she enrolled at NYU and went to live with them. I thought about going back home but this small-town girl knew that her calling was destined to take her elsewhere. I left *"Bienvenido a refugio Seguro"* a different person with a new attitude. Margaret "Peggy" Smythe, was never going to be played again.

Remember that poem at the beginning? The lines were changed a little to fit the beginning of my story, but this is how the story ends:

> *If by chance, I ever be a star,*
> *I'll remember you though I may be far,*
> *All that fame and glory be,*

remember lover you will always have me.
You were with me when times were hard.
And when I felt insecure
you stood by me like a guard.
My mother said, I shouldn't let you go,
When it comes to what's best
Mothers sure do know.

My family wasn't the only one I reconnected with. I also reconnected with lover (Brian). I wrote this poem before I left, and I gave it to him. You see it was the intentions of this small-town girl to become a star and come back and marry that boy, but life got in the way of true love. But Brian, sweet Brian waited all these years for me and guess who became the star and guess who still wanted to marry little messed-up, cleaned-up, restored me?

TARRENT-'AUTHUR' HENRY

The name could have been Margaret,
Jane or Sue, It could have been me,
it could have been you.
When life gives you lemons you made lemonade,
For a day's work you expect to get paid.
It's almost like a punch in the gut,
Or have you ever been stuck in a rut?

Have you ever wanted something really bad,
But someone else got it and it made you mad?

Ever look in a mirror and the face you see,
Looks nothing like you but exactly like me?

You went to your car and all the tires were flat,
Have you ever thought you saw a puddy tat?

Have you ever watched a movie
for the umpteenth time,
Ever see a batter miss the hit and run sign?

Like a college student and a bachelor's degree,
The cost of education always comes with a fee.

Like a snowball don't belong on a hot day in July,
But baseball, hotdogs and apple pie.

The name might be Dave, Bob or Lee,
Turn the page and start reading Chapter Three.

Chapter Three

"PUBLIC SAXOPHONE"

"I get stoned and I can't go home I'm calling long distance on a public saxophone......" (Midnight Lightning – Jimi Hendrix)

Some people go through life without you ever knowing their name, this is one of those stories:

Born to a crack addicted mother, the first name on his birth certificate having been left blank because she was so stoned out of her mind that after giving birth to this bouncy brown baby boy, she snuck out of the emergency room because she needed to get high.

Boy Doe didn't cry when he was born in fact the doctors and nurses thought he was still born when he came out of the womb of his young, scared, crack addicted mother who never gave her name or where she came from.

When a woman that is pregnant uses crack, the baby's oxygen supply is cut off. In Boy Doe's case, his mother had just smoked crack and being in the later stages of her pregnancy the living fetus began to kick madly as he was being strangled by each inhale of this deadly poison. It was a miracle that she gave birth, and he was able to survive.

> You didn't want me but I'm here,
> And there is nothing you can do about it.
> You can run and you can hide but I'm here,

And there is nothing you can do about it.

Mama did you see me, did you ever look at me?
Did you even hold me or kiss me?
Mama I'm here and I'm scared.

Daddy, where are you daddy?
Aren't you proud to have a son?
Daddy did you even know, did you even ask?
Daddy I'm here and I'm frightened.

Mama do you love me?
Daddy are you proud of me?
Mama won't you look at me?
Mama? Daddy? Mama?

I keep having these *dreams*. Ever since I was a small child, I have had these dreams. And the headaches and heartaches that always follow. Then the nausea and dizziness. Oh, if I could only die.

No home, no name,
They call me scarecrow,
They say I have no brain.

No family, nayer a friend,
They say I'm anti-social,
But that all depends.

Crack baby, crack baby,
That's all I ever hear,
Boy Doe, Boy Doe,
The name rings in my ear.

You good for nothing,
Throw away child,
Your mama didn't want you,

Cause you're so wild.

In and out of foster care,
You juvenile delinquent,
All you do is stare.

Nobody wants you,
Never did,
You'll amount to nothing,
You throwaway kid.

Well, it's time to get up and at'um. I have been on my own for the past seventeen years. On the day I turned eighteen they had my stuff packed and waiting for me at the front desk. They basically said, *"good riddance to me and don't let the door hit you on the way out."*

I left with the clothes on my back, and I have never looked back or had any regrets. I could write a book about my time in the system where I spend the first eighteen years of my life. I watched as other boys and girls were adopted and received new homes and forever families. But nobody wanted to take a chance with a crack baby whose mother didn't love enough to even give a name.

I was able to find work to earn a few dollars. Never had a problem getting something to eat or somewhere to sleep. I spent my days moving around and taking in the sights and sounds of the mean streets. I use to help this dude who ran a hippie joint where I was introduced to this cool black guitar player who I never heard of, named Jimi Hendrix. Max said, *"You kinda look like him, now all you need is a Git- tar"*

So, I saved up some money and went to the pawn shop and bought a lead guitar. Unfortunately, I may have looked like Hendrix, unfortunately, I didn't play nothing like him. Within six months I had returned the guitar to the pawn shop and got a quarter of what I originally paid, what a rip-off so I decide to pawn it instead and hold onto the ticket.

A cat told me about this jazz club that was looking for some help cleaning and bussing tables at night for food, a place to sleep and tips so I jumped on it. During the day, I was able to do my little hustle and from 9:00 to the wee hours I worked at the club where I was exposed to jazz for the first time. Listening to Byrd Charlie Parker and John Coltrane. Stan Getz, Dexter Gordon and Wayne Shorter playing the sax. And when I heard the Prez Lester Young, I was blown away. I had to have me a sax.

I met a sax player named Skeet, who had a heroin habit and one day he needed money and offered to sell me his sax for a fix. I use to run errands for the musicians from time to time when they needed a little something, something, so I took him up on his offer and bought his sax for a 20 dollar hit.

When I got my hands on the sax for the first time, I kissed every key as soon as my lips touched the mouthpiece, and I began to blow into my brass beauty and the sweetest sound could be heard. I had found the key to my happiness.

About a week later I heard a loud rap on my door, *"Open the door, Boy, I need to talk to you!"* It was Sam the owner or the Jazz club and Skeet. *"Yeah, that's it over there. That's my baby"*, *as he pointed to the sax that I bought from him for a 20 dollar hit. Sam shouted, "Give him his sax and get out!" I said, "Wait a minute Bossman, I bought the sax from Skeet!" Sam stared me down and said, "You got any proof like a bill of sale?" "Ask Skeet, to roll up his arm because he sold it to me for a 20-dollar hit of skag."*

Birds of a feather flock together. It was a black man's word against a white man's lie and we all know that the white man's lie always wins. I was out of twenty dollars, out of a sax, out of a place to eat and sleep and out of a job.

Why does bad news always seem to travel fast? I stopped by Max to see if he needed any help and he told me not to come around anymore. It seems Sam had put the word out about me, the wrong word.

I never meant to speak a wrong word about anybody, but it seems like over the course of my life that people who have wronged me ended up dead. Two days later, Skeet was found in the same room at Sam's that I have been staying in with a hypodermic needle in his arm having injected himself with some bad dope. And the jazz club was raided and shut down. That bad news travelled even faster, and people started to feel sorry for me. But it was too late because I had already left town a day earlier.

The cats who played at the jazz club, knew Skeet and knew me and pulled out and asked me to come with them. It was a no brainer for me because I knew I was washed up in Ragtime, City. So, we went on the Greyhound bus to Boomtown. The guys used me to run errands and to keep a lookout. They even taught me how to play the sax and read music though I was better at hearing and playing than reading notes.

We had been on the road for about two years when I got my big chance, Big Clarence got really sick and had to stay in the hospital and they were short an alto sax and since they knew I knew all the parts I was asked to fill in. I took to the stage like I belonged and blended in with the quintet. Consisting of a trumpet, alto, tenor, bass and drums and we were sometimes accompanied by piano.

When Big Clarence got out of the hospital and found out that the quintet was doing better without him and that I had taken his place, he blew his top and threaten to kill me. One night after we finished our first set, I walked into the mens room and Big Clarence was waiting for me, I heard the first shot and that is all I remember.

I kept hearing voices but seeing no one. I heard somebody praying then silence. I remember seeing a bright light and harmonic singing like in the movie, *"Cabin In the Sky"*. Then everything went completely black.

When I woke up, I was in a sterile white room wearing a hospital gown under clean sheets. There was an IV in my arm and it hurt when I tried to move. I couldn't speak and there was a black nun sitting in a chair crocheting and praying. A doctor came in and looked at my chart and said, *"1/8 of an inch more and we wouldn't be having this conversation"*, as he looked me in the eye. *"My name is Doctor Savage, and I just performed the surgery that saved your life. You are lucky to be alive young man."*

I remained in the hospital for about two weeks regaining my strength and trying to figure things out. That black nun just sat in the chair, crocheting, and praying without missing a beat. Every time

I looked; she was there, never saying a word to me. But I sensed her presence and needed her strength if I hoped to survive.

I imagined and thought to myself, maybe she's, my mother? My long-lost mother?

Mama do you see me, do you ever look at me?
Do you want to hold me or kiss me?
Mama I'm here and I'm scared.

Then I would always fall into a deep sleep and have the sweetest dreams.

The day of my discharge, I awoke to find the chair empty. The room quiet. I asked the discharge nurse about the crocheting, praying nun and she looked at me like I had lost my mind.

I had no clothes to wear so I was provided with some hand-me downs. As I slowly began to get dressed, I noticed I had everything but a hat in the bag. It was wintertime and I knew it would be cold. When I walked back to the bed laying on my pillow was a crocheted bucket hat, I hadn't lost my mind.

I was given my discharge papers and made my way through the hospital lobby and into the streets. I took the hat from my hand where I was holding it and before I could put it on my head, a card fell out which said: *"Please wait for me in the lobby if you want to receive good news."*

Boy Doe took a seat by the main entrance and waited and waited. After about a half hour a man approached me and motioned for me to follow him. We got into a van, and he took me to the place where I would spend the next two years.

When I arrived, I was warmly greeted and given a hot meal which I surely needed. I was assigned a room and given a voucher to get the things I needed from the supply chain. I returned to my room and sitting in the middle was a familiar case inside it contained the most beautiful brass saxophone I had ever seen.

"Do you like it?", a man with a raspy sounding voice spoke as he came inside my room and introduced himself, *"Hi, my name is Ben, welcome to your new home. You can stay as long as you like."*

I found out that that quintet and the man that shot me, Big Clarence had made their way over to Europe and were making a name for themselves in Paris, France. Funny, the police never questioned me about the shooting, so no one was ever charged. My life up to this point was no bowl of cherries, I could write a book about all the bad things that had happened to me. I even wrote a song that goes:

> *Everything happens to me,*
> *Oh, everything happens to me,*
> *Why Oh, why Oh,*
> *Does everything happen to me?*

During my two years at the mission, I had the opportunity to be around people that understood me. There was a motley crew of personalities there all trying to find their place in this world. I found mine through music, playing the sax and I discovered I had talent as an artist.

I learned that it was okay to be myself and I learned how to get in touch with my feelings. I learned how to swim, box and wrestle to release tension and I made some forever friends.

My last year I spent as a paid-staff member, and I would still be there today if this didn't happen. I had taken a group of autistic children on an outing which involved boating and swimming. We all were in a water raft, wearing life jackets and strapped in tight. There were eight of us in the boat and we were having the time of our lives.

As we were battling the water and the waves, we hit a rock. It didn't seem like a big deal at first but for some reason the raft became pinned and just liked that flipped over and we all were in the water. Myself, Rennie and six autistic children. I acted quickly and instructed Rennie to move the kids to land as I freed them, some were under the water. One by one I was able to free them as five kids moved to shore, Rennie signaled me that there was one more still trapped. I dove under the water and into the overturned raft to free the last child, but it was already too late. His body was motionless, and it floated to the surface. I was distraught, I was devastated as I guided the lifeless body to the shore.

I spent the next two weeks reliving this horrible tragedy. All the joy and satisfaction that I had achieved vanished overnight because of that one incident. I kept hearing this over and over again inside my mind until it tormented me:

No home, no name,
They call me scarecrow,
They say I have no brain.

No family, nayer a friend,
They say I'm anti-social,
But that all depends.

Crack baby, crack baby,
That's all I ever hear,
Boy Doe, Boy Doe,
The name rings in my ear.

You good for nothing,
Throw away child,

Your mama didn't want you,
Cause you're so wild.

In and out of foster care,
You juvenile delinquent,
All you do is stare.

Nobody wants you,
Never did,
You'll amount to nothing,
You throwaway kid.

After a thorough investigation, it was determined that no criminal charges would be filed against me and that I was not negligent. But the parents of the autistic boy wanted their pound of flesh, so they filed a personal injury claim against me, and the mission and they won a substantial judgement. I was asked to resign my position and am never allowed to work with or around children ever again.

> *Just when it seemed like,*
> *I was about to turn the corner,*
> *Just when it seemed like,*
> *I found where I belonged,*
> *Just when it seemed like,*
> *I finally had a future,*
> *I was wrong.*

I left the mission with only the clothes on my back and my sax. I hitched a ride to the bus depot and bought a ticket as far away from life as I could on a one-way ticket. I was damned if I did and damned if I don't. I met a man who was travelling with me and every time I took a seat, he'd sit down beside me as quiet as a church mouse. All he seemed to do is read and sleep.

When we had to switch buses for the last leg of the long ride across America, I purposely boarded last and headed to a seat I spotted in the rear of the bus, I had my sax in my hand and was about to place it under the seat when yours truly came up behind me and took the seat next to me. I looked at him with my death stare and he smiled at me and spoke for the first time, He introduced himself as Pete Morgan and began to share his brief bio, it seemed that we had a lot in common.

Pete, was running away too, seems he got caught up in a scandal at his church and was told to leave and to never return. We became fast friends and decided to form an alliance which we still have to this day. We decided that he would preach, and I would play and that's how we made a living. Pete was like a guardian angel, he gave me my first Bible and taught me how to pray.

Our favorite tune was *"When The Saints Go Marching In"* and while I played my sax to attract the crowd, Pete would deliver his short message and many got saved. I even gave my life to Christ during one of the meetings.

I surrender all,
I surrender all,
All to thee, my blessed Savior,
I surrender all.

I soon learned to play that song as well and we soon began to empty out the bars and brothels which didn't sit well with the people who made their money selling sin.

Pete was an early riser and one morning as he was taking his prayer walk, he was accosted by some angry men who beat him within an inch of his life. I was awaked by screams and then shouts as I quickly got myself together and looked out my window at the crowd that had formed. Then I heard sirens and ambulances and police cars were everywhere. Then somebody said, *"that's the preacher!"*

I ran down the stairs and out into the street and pushed through the crowd. I kneeled and for the first time in my life I began to pray for someone other than myself. I prayed words that I never heard before and then I heard a moan and I thought I heard Pete say, *"Amen!"*

At that moment the ambulance came, and they let me go with him to the hospital. I waited patiently as the doctors did all they could to save him, but I knew for the first time that it wasn't doctors but prayer that makes all the difference. To make a long story short, Pete survived.

The police began to question me about Pete. I could only tell them what I knew, his name, Pete Morgan and that he was a preacher. Turns out he was more than that. Pete was a wanted man. There was a warrant out for his arrest, and I felt so bad because in my innocence I gave his secret *(that he kept even from me)* away. If he survived, Pete would be going away for a long time.

I walked the streets like a zombie. The only friend I ever had, now this. I began to talk to God and for the first time I entered a church. A baptism service was going on and I asked to be baptized and I was. When I came out of the water, I felt like a reborn man, I had love to give from the touch of my hand. I told the Pastor what had happened, and he promised to visit and pray for Pete.

The bad news is that Pete survived but he was beaten so severely that when he fell his spine was severed so he was partially paralyzed. The good news is that the charges against Pete were dropped due to his condition and circumstance. Today, Pete is in a home that cares for paralytics telling everyone he can about God's mercy and His grace.

I bet you're probably saying to yourself, does anything good happen in this man's life? Well, I saved the best for last.

I took my show on the road again and I found myself in a city that was full of life. I noticed how much the panhandlers were making on the streets plying their trades and soon found myself among them.

I would set up shop and entertain the people all day playing jazz and special requests on my saxophone. By now, I had moved on from the alto and now played soprano.

By day, I played in the village and by night I played in front of a club that featured jazz after 9. I would play outside the club for tips to help attract the crowd and oftentimes I'd grab someone to sing from the passersbys.

I noticed this young girl and her mother in the crowd from time to time. I noticed that the mother often left the girl who looked no more than ten close by me in front of the club and then returned, always in a hurry and scurried off.

One night I was playing, *"God, bless the child that got its own."* And this little alto/soprano blew me and every one that heard her sing away. Tens and twenties began to fill my sax case. I never seen so many tens and twenties fill my case. I must have easily made several hundred dollars.

Her mother came back but this time I stopped her and asked her name, *"Olivia",* she said, shyly. *"Let's go, Little b----",* her mother said. I called her back and put the money from my case into her pocket which her mother quickly snatched, left Olivia and headed in the other direction.

Since it was time for sets to begin inside the club, I packed up my sax and looked at Olivia's sullen face. *"When was the last time you ate?"* *"Yesterday morning,"* she said. *"How 'bout us getting some-*

thing to eat?" and off we went to Sophie's Spoon, I choose Sophie's because we could sit by the window and see her mother when she came back to get her. Ten o'clock, eleven, o'clock. Finally, at 11:45 her mother came hustling down the street like her pants were on fire. We stepped out of Sophie's to meet her, and she nearly knocked us over. *"Mama!"*, Olivia cried. You could tell her mother was really booted, she snatched Olivia by the hand and brushed past me.

I went back inside to talk with Sophie, *"That girl's mother is like the walking dead. Instead of getting better, she is getting worse. I feel so sorry for that little girl. She doesn't belong on these streets."* I was shooting the breeze with Sophie when she punched me and said, *"Look!"* I stared out the window. *"She done sold her daughter to that nasty pimp!"*

I tore out of Sophie's and stepped in front of this tall black muscular dude and looked at Olivia and then looked him in the eye and said, *"Where you are going with her man?"* *"Are you looking to get hurt,* Public Saxophone, *go play your music and stay out of grown folk's business. This is between her mother and me"*. *"How much?"*, I said, *"How much?"* Sophie had walked out with her cell phone in her hand. The pimp let Olivia go and she ran to Sophie as I stepped to the side with this monster and paid the price. He didn't want any trouble only his money.

Sophie closed early and took Olivia upstairs and got her ready for bed. Tomorrow was Saturday so she could sleep late and maybe by then we could sort things out and see how we can get her settled.

When I got up the next morning, Olivia was asleep, but Sophie was in the kitchen doing her thing. Somebody has got to feed those hungry stomachs and nurse those nasty hangovers.

Soon the detectives made their way into Sophie's and what they had to say was what we didn't want to hear. Olivia's mother was found dead

Olivia's grandparents were contacted. It was amazing because this was the first time, they ever saw one other. They stayed just long enough to arrange the funeral and take their only granddaughter, Olivia back with them.

I was able to spend some time with Olivia before she left and she promised me that she would be a good girl, keep on singing and would visit me every summer. Her grandparents said, they would do just that. But how many of you know that adults sometimes lie? You don't have to tell me; I am a living witness.

Olivia was in my prayers each and every day. I never stopped praying for her or losing hope that I would ever see her again. She gave me a reason for living, a reason to keep going on. Her grandparents moved so all the letters came back, return to sender. They never allowed me to call so we lost contact.

One year, two years, three years went by. Each time I played, "God bless the child....", I thought of her.

Four years, five years, six years went by, and Sophie opened Olivia's Oven, she thought of her.

Seven years, eight years, nine years went by, and I was outside the jazz club doing my usual when I heard an acapella voice singing: "Papa may have, Mama may have but God bless the child that's got its own..."

I looked up and I saw Sophie arm and arm with Olivia now all grown up and immediately I switched my key to accompany her sweet soprano voice. The club emptied and people stopped in their tracks on the street to hear that voice that sounded like sleighbells in the snow, in summertime.

And, oh you know the rest of the story. Olivia signed an exclusive record deal and recording contract. She hired me to be her music director and Sophie got out of the food business, sold her restaurants, and became her manager.

And her first album, she dedicated to me and called it: "Public Saxophone".

TARRENT-'AUTHUR' HENRY

I'm speaking to you,
Who never had a home,
Who never had a friend,
Keep living.

I'm speaking to you,
Who has given up hope,
About to take a rope,
Keep living.

I'm speaking to you,
Who forgot how to dream,
And are letting off some steam,
Keep living.

Chapter Four

"THE TRAPEZOID"
("a quadrilateral with only one pair of parallel sides.")

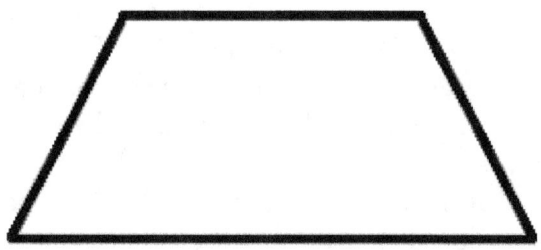

I looked to the sky and I wondered why?
The sixteen letter of the Greek alphabet,
Is transliterated as pi.

Then I looked beyond your point of view,
Do you see what I'm seeing?
Or has time just been renewed?

He has the deepest pockets in the whole wide world, and she is the most beautiful girl that I have ever seen. Geovanni said to himself as he thumbed through a magazine. He was patiently waiting.

Geovanni was looking for work. He had been out of work for two years. Today, he said to himself, *this is the day they have to hire me.*

The receptionist called his name after he waited almost three hours and said, *"Sir, I'm very sorry but all the positions have been filled today but you are welcomed to come back tomorrow and try again."*

He reached into his jacket and pulled out a handgun and pointed it at the young woman's head and pulled the trigger. He didn't stop shooting until he ran out of bullets. Six people either laid wounded or dead. The gunman escaped and is still at large.

Geovanni heard the news as it flashed across the screen. It was the same office he had left only ten minutes earlier. He thought to himself, *I could have been the gunman or one of the victims.*

He took a minute to make the sign of the cross and thank his deceased mother for his name which means, *"God is gracious"*.

Geovanni never had it easy, born in Brazil, his mother brought him to America when he was ten. Not being able to speak English, she struggled to make ends meet and make a life for her and her son.

Though fluent in Portuguese, Spanish and English, Geovanni struggled with stuttering which made it hard for him to communicate. He was called and labelled a dummy when in fact he was a stuttering genius.

He often collected bottles and cans and lived in back alleys and slept in old, abandoned cars. He was often the victim of beatings and verbal abuse because of his perceived handicap. Many nights he cried himself to sleep missing his mother, the only woman who ever really loved him.

As he walked past the Roman Catholic Church, he went inside as was his normal custom to offer his alms and sit in one of the back pews. But today was not going to be like any other day in Geo's life.

I heard a voice say loud and clear,
Don't look down,
Or let your eyes shed a tear.

Then something unusual happened to me,
A Talking Spirit
Entered me.

I got up to leave the church and Father Richie spoke to me and I answered him in a voice I did not recognize. He looked at me and smiled, *"God has worked a miracle in answer to your departed mother's prayers."*

And just like that Geovanni Mauricio Nascimento was able to speak fluently, and doors began to open for him that no man could shut. He went from a stuttering dummy to a trilingual genius.

There are some things in life,
That are hard to avoid.
You just entered the world,
Of the Trapezoid..........

Mabel Thornton is a God-fearing woman. Ever since she was a little girl growing up in the deep south, she knew God. She was saved and baptized at the age of three and served her church faithfully.

A lot of people in Mabel's position would have given up hope but as she sat waiting, praying, she hadn't lost her faith.

The apartment building that she lived in for fifty years was sold and Mabel was given a 30-day eviction notice. Mabel hadn't saved much instead preferring to give her money to the church and whoever else who was down on their luck. Now when she needed the church most, all the preachers could do was say, *"We'll be praying for you, Mother Thornton."*

Mabel grabbed her big pocketbook and the only piece of luggage she had borrowed from a neighbor and took her last look at the apartment that she thought she would die in and thanked God and shut the door for the last time. *"Surely goodness and mercy shall follow me all the days of my life and I will dwell in the house of the Lord forever."* She said as she walked to the subway.

She took the token that a stranger had given to her the other day and placed in into the turnstile and slowly entered the train station as she proudly took her bags, singing as she waited on the platform for the "A" train.

Nobody knows the trouble I've seen but Jesus.
But through it all, I've learned to trust Him.
God has a purpose; God has a plan.
He didn't bring me this far just to leave me.

The crowed "A" train came chugging into the station. Mabel grabbed her bags and made her way through the open doors. An older gentleman offered Mabel his seat. She thanked him and let her weary body plop down into the hard gray subway seat.

The train was loud and noisy but that didn't bother Mabel as she was in deep conversation with God. You see, she had not a clue to where she was going or what to do. She rode to the last stop, Inwood (207th Street) in upper Manhattan, NY. She got back on and rode the downtown train that ended at Mott Avenue in Far Rockaway, NY just outside of Queens and Long Island.

Then she finally heard that still-small-voice which only comes from the Father and she now knew where she was headed. *"God always has a plan"*, she smiled.

The "A" roared into 42nd street – Port Authority Bus Terminal. This was the stop she heard in her spirit. She gathered herself, grabbed her things and slowly made her way to the open doors. She made her way down the platform to the ramp leading to the Bus Terminal.

While she was walking, she stopped to catch her breath and something told her to, *"look down"*, and there were two crumbled dollar bills lying at her feet. *"Thank you, Jesus"*, she said to herself. There was a little café on her left, so she stopped and purchased two bottles of water.

Mabel entered the Bus Terminal, stopped, and took a seat near the arrival and departure sign. She opened one bottle of water and sipped until she had to use the bathroom. *"Lord, I'm trusting you and waiting on you. I have no money and no place to go, and you promised me since I was a little girl that you would never leave me nor forsake me."*

She came back from the ladies room and began to smile as she headed toward Greyhound bus 1011 leaving at 8:45 pm to Miami, Florida. She reached the gate and stood in line. The passengers began to board. Mabel was praying as she reached the front of the line. The driver asked for her ticket. She explained to the driver that she was there by *"divine appointment "*and she had to be on this bus.

The driver looked at her quizzically, asked her to step to the side and proceeded to take the next rider.

By this time Mabel was in deep prayer, praying in her prayer language and just as the driver was about to close the luggage compartment and depart from the terminal. A tall man dressed in a black suit hurried to the front of the bus and said, *"Driver, wait a minute, I have a ticket for a passenger, I don't know who it is, but we can't leave until they are on this bus".*

The driver looked at the man and then looked at Mabel, then astonishly said, *"I guess you were right, ma'am." "May I take your bag?"*

The man in the black suit helped Mabel unto the bus and ushered her to her seat and she took her place by the window. She closed her eyes and began to pray and thank God. The tall man introduced himself as Reverend Charles C. Wright and the two became quickly acquainted as they had the same Father.

Mabel shared her life story and when she got to the part of how she happened to be on this bus it really got Reverend Wright's interest. He asked Mabel to look at the ticket's destination. *"Does that mean anything to you?"* The ticket said: **Florence, S.C.** Tears welled up in her big brown eyes.

"I was born outside Florence and now God is bringing Mabel Thornton back home." "Excuse me, did you say the name Thornton?" "Yes, Mabel Louise Thornton," did I say something wrong; you look like you seen the Holy Ghost!"

"Mabel Thornton, I don't know where to begin. Does the name, Shirley, mean anything to you"? "Shirley Louise"? she stammered. *"Yes, Shirley Louise Thornton, ma'am!" "That's my daughter's name but I haven't seen Shirl in about five years. We had a big falling out and I threw her out of the house and told her I never wanted to see her again."*

"Well, ma'am, God had other ideas." "You see, we were just recently led to purchase this mother/daughter house (two fully equipped apartments in a one-family house) it's beautiful. One of your neighbors got in touch with one of Shirl's friend's and I came to New York to bring you

home. But you had already left but I trusted God and followed his directions and now we are going to be one complete blessed family."

Mabel began to cry. How many of you know that *"God news"* travels fast? The driver pulled over the bus and got on the intercom. He had a rich baritone voice and began to sing: *"Victory is mine…"* Other passengers on the bus came over to offer their thanks and well wishes as they had witnessed a miracle right before their very eyes.

The Greyhound soon got back on the road and Mabel fell asleep. The bus arrived in Florence at 2:00 pm. The skies were blue, and they were greeted by a cool breeze. Reverend Wright exited the bus to retrieve their bags. Mabel, took his hand as she stepped off the bus took in a deep breath and sighed, *"Home!"*

Some store up treasures,
Money, cars and homes,
But when you die,
You die alone.

Rich man, poor man,
All bleed the same,
But it's the heart's condition,
That gives one a great name.

Willie Mack was a master auto mechanic. Each morning he would stagger out of bed, grab his tools and head out to his designated spot on the street where he plied his craft. The old, abandoned car that he used was usually an old clunker that was beyond repair, but Willie often used it to store parts and equipment that he used to make the repairs.

Willie honed his craft in the military as a wheeled vehicle mechanic. Ever since he could remember he was always taking something apart and putting it back together. His father and grandfather worked with their hands and passed their craft down to him. There was nothing Willie couldn't take apart and put back together.

This morning, Fonzie Fritz was waiting for Willie with his motorcycle. He had a clutch problem which Willie promised to take care of first thing. Willie use to have a good job working for General Motors but a problem that he developed while in the service kept him from holding down steady employment.

Willie Mack liked to tip the elbow and often fixed vehicles for the price of a pint of hooch. By noon, he would be drunk as a skunk. You would find him laid out in that old, abandoned car, talking gibberish.

If you sobered him up, he could tell you how to do most any repair, but his hands were too shaky, and he would drop the tools if he tried to do it himself.

Willie lived alone and his brother Jimmie would always stop by when he got off work and carry his big brother home to his little back room that he lived in next door to the filling station. Jimmie worked construction and started work at the crack of dawn and was usually home by five. He hated the smell of hooch.

Jimmie got to the car to retrieve his big brother. Willie wasn't moving. Jimmie shook and called his name, but Willie didn't budge. Jimmie quickly dialed 9-1-1 and an ambulance was soon dispatched to take Willie to the hospital. The doctors pumped his stomach for around twenty minutes before one of them came out and said that Willie was in a coma.

Gillie Mack, was on the phone when he suddenly felt an urge to end the call and pray. Gillie got down on his hands and knees in his office and prayed like never before. When he got off the floor, the phone suddenly rang. It was his baby brother Jimmie. Jimmie told him, what happened to his middle brother, Willie.

Gillie, immediately got off the phone and jumped in his truck and headed to the hospital praying all the way. Neither Jimmie or Willie were praying men but Gillie was a man after God's own heart and he now knew why he was suddenly led to get off the phone and go to his knees in prayer. Gillie was the only one that knew at that time, God's got this.

Gillie pulled into the parking lot and walked into County hospital. He asked, where he could find his brother Willie Mack. When he got to ICU, Jimmie was pacing back and forth with his hands on his head. When he saw his big brother, Gillie, he ran over to him and hugged him for dear life. The brothers had been estranged so they embraced for a long time

"God's got this", little brother. "He's had his hand on you and Willie for a long time." Jimmie bowed his head and said, *"Gillie, show me how to ask Him into my life?"* and then and there, Gillie lead Jimmie in a prayer of repentance as he asked Christ into his heart and life.

The doctor met them as they walked back into ICU. *"Are you the Mack brothers?"* "We sure are, "said Gillie. *"The prognosis for your brother is not good..."* before the doctor could finish making his statement, Gillie cut in, *"No, disrespect Doc, but have you ever witnessed a miracle?"*

Before the doctor could say another word, Gillie motioned for him to follow he and Jimmie into Willie's room. Gillie placed his hands on Willie and told Jimmie to do the same and they both shouted together, **"IN THE NAME OF JESUS, RISE UP OUT OF THIS HERE BED!"**

Then suddenly Willie's lifeless body came to attention like a soldier and Willie's eyes opened wide as if he'd seen something that no other living human being had ever seen. ***"I'M BACK, I'M BACK, I'M ALIVE, I'M ALIVE!" "JIMMIE, OH MY GOSH, GILLIE, I WANNA LIVE, I WANNA LIVE!!!***

The doctors and staff looked on in amazement as the Mack brothers had their little reunion. Gillie led Willie in a prayer of repentance and acceptance, and the three brothers walked out of that hospital, leaping, dancing, and praising God!

I looked to the sky and I wondered why?
The sixteen letter of the Greek alphabet,
Is transliterated as pi.

Then I looked beyond your point of view,
Do you see what I'm seeing?
Or has time just been renewed?

I heard a voice say loud and clear,
Don't look down,
Or let your eyes shed a tear.
Then something unusual happened to me,
A Talking Spirit
Entered me.

There are some things in life,
That are hard to avoid.
You just entered the world,
Of the Trapezoid..........

Her Father named her Prunella. Her aunties said, she looked like a baby gorilla. Her mother died after giving birth due to severe bleeding. So, her father was left to raise her alone with the help of her aunties.

Her Father tried to give her all the love she needed. But her aunties, well they were another story. The Father was tall, brown, and handsome but Prunella favored her deceased mom, she was dark and homely.

Prunella learned at an early age that she was different from the others. While her cousins were favored by her grandparents because of their light skin. She was often referred to as the *"bogger baby."*

Despite all the teasing and favoritism, Prunella always knew she was loved. Her daddy, Otis, always made sure to let his baby know that she was his chocolate delight and how he loved chocolate.

While her cousins were enrolled in piano and dance. Prunella often stayed in her room and pretended she was Cinderella. This kept her going day by day and helped her cope with her condescending aunties and cousins.

When Prunella was five, her father started dated a woman who would later become her stepmother. She had two sons that were ten and twelve. Otis and Donna got married after dating a little over a year and moved to a new town and city far away from her grandparents, aunties, and cousins.

Prunella was now six and her daddy made sure that she had her own room. The boys, Trevor and Travis shared a room. They were hoping to become one big happy family.

Otis got a good job that paid him a lot of money but it took him away from home a lot and he mostly worked the graveyard shift from 7:00 to 7:00. Donna also worked from 9:00 to 5:00 so it meant that Travis now 13 had the responsibility to watch over Trevor and Prunella.

Travis and Trevor often use to bully Prunella and each time she would complain to her stepmother she would tell her to stop exaggerating and stop being such a cry baby. Since her daddy worked the night shift, she hardly got to see him anymore, so she pretended that she was Cinderella.

Prunella started the first grade. Her teacher, Ms. Graham took a liking to her and made her feel like a special student. Ms. Graham helped her develop a talent she never knew she had, singing.

When her daddy, Otis heard her sing for the first time at the assembly, he couldn't contain himself. He was so proud of his only daughter. He was sure to let everyone know that she was his baby girl.

As Prunella got older, her voice got stronger and better. Prunella, the baby gorilla as she was called by her aunties and cousins was now, "Ella Prunella" after Ella Fitzgerald. And most times just "Ella".

Prunella began to grow tall like her daddy. Her skin chocolate brown. She was growing up to be quite a young lady. Her stepmother began to get jealous because she felt her daddy was paying more attention to "Ella" than her.

Otis wasn't having it so he sent "Ella", back home to live with her grandparents for the summer. He figured this would give him time to work things out with Donna.

"Ella" soon became their favorite, and her aunties and cousins couldn't get enough of their new found celebrity niece and cousin.

Donna and Otis would have some heated arguments. It was usually Donna that was the most vocal. Trevor and Travis who were now 15 and 17 often jumped to their mother's defense. But this argument was much different from any encounter they had had before.

Apparently, this time someone had called the police and before anyone could react. Six police cars and ten officers had surrounded the house and were knocking at the door with drawn guns.

"POLICE – OPEN THE DOOR" was the first command. Trevor, who was closest to the door was shot first. Donna screamed before another shot rang out and hit Otis. All in all, twenty shots were fired, and two people apparently laid dead.

When the Washington family got the news. They whole family was devastated. There was not a dry eye in the entire house. "Ella", was still at choir rehearsal and hadn't gotten home yet. Grandaddy Washington called the church and told the Pastor the news. Pastor Jaxson said, he would bring "Ella" home with the deacons and console the family.

"Ella", took the news hard. She ran into her room and closed the door and pretended to be Cinderella.

"This whole thing just makes no sense, Pastor. No sense.", Grandaddy Washington said, as he paced up and down the living room wearing out the carpet.

Then everybody heard a voice like a choir of angels singing from Prunella's room and she walked out and said, *"Daddy will live and not die and declare the glory of the Lord!"* And then she walked back into her room and totally collapsed.

The phone in the house rang and it was Donna. Papa Washington picked it up. Donna was frantic on the other end, *"Papa Washington, Papa Washington, you won't believe what just happened!* "They brought *Otis and Trevor in and pronounced them dead and then suddenly we all heard a voice, to me it sounded like Prunella, and Otis and Trevor bodies both began to shake and they got off those gurneys and started screaming and shouting and praising Jesus like they just lost their minds. It's a miracle!* "A freaking miracle! Glory to God!"

Papa Washington had put the phone on speaker, so everyone heard what had occurred.

Then he said, *"when Otis named her, I asked him why in tar-nation do you want to name her Prunella. He looked me in the eye and said, Daddy, because God says she's special and her name means "Heal All."*

TARRENT-'AUTHUR' HENRY

Just a second,
Away from a minute,
Circling round,
The universe.

Sitting and staring,
At four walls blank.
Placing a deposit
In an empty bank.

Driving in a car,
That flies like a plane.
Being diagnosed
As totally insane.

Then it appeared,
Like out of nowhere.

Tried to follow it
But blip it was gone.

Ever try to drink
Dry water
On shaky ground?

Or eat a piece
Of fruit
Without making a sound?

Experience the obvious,
Contained in a glass.
Or being demoted
To an upper class?

HOW TO TURN OFF YOUR BRAIN AND LISTEN TO GOD

Like a feeling
You never
Saw before.

Like a sound
You taste
Before the roar.

There are some things in life,
That are hard to avoid.
And one of those things is
The Trapezoid..................

Chapter Five

"MOSES AARON"

("God will always watch over His children, but the fool will have to watch out for himself.")

Put in prison for a crime that he didn't commit and where have we heard this story before? A young black man arrested, tried, and convicted based on circumstantial evidence. A victim of systemic racism.

Moses Aaron was given the death sentence and placed on Death Row. There are currently 46 males on Death Row awaiting execution.

The jury returned a unanimous guilty verdict after deliberating for only six hours. Moses Aaron was led away in handcuffs and scheduled for sentencing.

When that day came, all eyes in the courtroom were on Moses as the judge announced the sentencing. Moses was handed the most severe punishment that he could have received, death by lethal injection.

As Moses was led away, trying to hold back the tears, his family ravaged by the worst possible news a family could ever expect to hear, he felt a sudden peace enter his heart.

Moses was placed in isolation and separated from the general prison population. He remained in his cell all day and was allowed an hour a day to leave his cell for exercise. He had a lot of time to think but he mostly dreamed.

It happened on a Friday night or early Saturday morning. Moses and some friends were out partying at a club till around 3 am. The crime was reported to have taken place at approximately 1 in the morning. According to the police report, a man fitting Moses' description broke into a home and in the process of committing burglary was surprised by the owner of the house. He subsequently subdued the victim and strangled and tortured he and his wife, leaving both dead before fleeing the scene.

Moses was one of a group of men rounded up and questioned about their whereabouts the night of the murder. The police were able to obtain evidence but none of it tied Moses to ever being at the crime scene.

As it would happen, one of Moses' friends that he was partying with that Friday night got arrested on a drug charge. The police made a deal with him that if he gave them information about who might have committed the murder, they would go easy on him and drop the marijuana charge. The fiend gave the cops the name, Moses Aaron.

Moses Aaron was 19 years old when he was arrested and preparing to go to a HBCU. Everyone said, *"Moses Aaron had a bright future."* He ran track and played football in High School, but he loved animals and was planning to go to veterinary school after getting his bachelor's degree.

The prosecution tried their case based on circumstantial evidence and an all-white jury. They presented Moses as a crazed animal and opportunist. The lead prosecutor used his size, 6' 4" muscular frame and ebony complexion to paint a picture and used his nickname, *"Panther"* which they added *"Black"* and portrayed him as a vicious killer.

Moses' friends his only alibi were intimidated by the police and when asked about Moses' whereabouts at the time of the murder one by one said," *either they couldn't remember if he was with them or if they even saw him on the night in question."*

His defense attorney told him that his goose was cooked and suggested that take a plea and cop to a lesser charge. But Moses and his family stuck by his innocence.

Moses was placed in a cell and the door was locked behind him. He began to survey his surroundings. A small bed with a mattress, white sheets, and a pillow on the right side. A toilet adjacent to the bed. The C.O. handed him a Bible that his Pastor had left for him. The Bible would become his best friend for the next 40 years.

My parents were determined that I was totally innocent though the newspapers had painted me and dubbed me as "The Black Panther Killer." They took a lot of abuse around town and soon had to move for their own safety. I felt for them as they felt for me.

During this time, I did a lot of writing, mostly letters then I started to keep a daily diary. My parents were able to get me a new attorney but the new one was just like the old one. But I never gave up hope.

I was not allowed any visitors but there was one C.O. who helped me through the process by sharing his faith with me. He often brought me reading material that gave me hope and he kept me up to date on what was going on in the outside world.

I celebrated my 21st birthday behind bars and since I was starting to get a little peach fuzz, I decided to not shave and to just let it grow. It was arranged that I could receive a call from my family. I had mixed feelings as I said, "Hello", to my mother for the first time in almost a year. It felt so good to hear my Pops strong steady voice and my baby brother, Keith, and baby sister Nell. But just like that my time was up and it was time to go back to my home away from home.

I woke up with a terrible pain in my stomach when I tried to sit up I couldn't. I called out to C.O. Addams and then I fell to the floor. When I woke up, I was in the infirmary in a lot of pain. It seems that terrible pain in my stomach was an appendicitis. I was diagnosed and rushed into surgery. The operation was a success and I spend two days there.

Moses was discharged and transferred back to his cell in isolation. The first news he received was his family would be coming to visit. He also learned that he would be eligible to take college courses and was given access to the prison library. His third attorney also was able to get permission for him to have a CD player to listen to prison approved music and teaching material.

The longer Moses remained in prison the more he began to feel at home. I don't know whether that was good or bad. Even some of the C.O.'s were talking amongst themselves that maybe Moses' didn't do the crimes he was convicted of and some of them began to give him special privileges within the rules.

I began to pour myself into my education. I decided if I had any hope of ever getting out of this place I needed to study the law for myself, so I took every course as it became available and even began to correspond with some outside people who were interested in my case and helping me prove my innocence.

Around this time, I was given the opportunity to meet with a chaplain once a week and I consented and started to meet with Chaplain Henry. We were scheduled to meet for an hour every Thursday but sometimes the C.O. on duty would extend the time. It felt good to talk to someone from the outside world and to share what I was going through on my world inside.

Chaplain Henry was concerned for me about my sexuality, and we broached that topic and he suggested for me to have a pen pal and gave me the name and address of a young woman that took an interest in wanting to get to know me. I took the information and forgot all about it and all about her.

Prison can be a lonely place. Sometimes the easiest thing to do is not to think at all. The days, the weeks, the months, the years go by, and the only constant is you and that prison cell. But you must find a way to hold on to your sanity. You mustn't give up hope. You must continue to dream.

I was given permission to attend Chapel for the first time. We would be meeting on Wednesday, and I was told that there would be both men and women in attendance though we would be separated and not able to mingle.

I was escorted in by a C.O. and surprised that I was allowed to remain unrestrained but there was one C.O. for every inmate. There were three male and five female inmates in attendance. Chaplain Henry conducted the service, and he had a singer with him. She was certainly a sight for my sore eyes, and she sang like a hummingbird. He introduced her as Evangelist Wotton. And I thought to myself where I had seen that name before.

After the service, we were escorted back to our respected cell blocks. I couldn't wait to get back to my cell and go through my notebook. There it was the same place I put it over three months ago, Alice Wotton.

Moses began to receive a letter from Alice at least once a week. As soon as one came, Moses read it and responded in the blink of an eye. He enjoyed getting a female perspective on things. She sent him a picture and he placed it on the small desk that he had been issued for his books and CD player.

Alice's letters helped Moses to keep his focus on God and of one day being exonerated and going back to living a life with a wife, house, kids, and a great career. Her letters help to make that dream appear alive.

Moses now looked forward to Wednesdays and Thursdays. Though Alice never came back to Chapel again. He enjoyed the presence of other souls like his that were lost and forgotten but each week looked forward to this gathering as they became one spirit.

The storm was so severe that all the inmates were to be prepared for emergency evacuation. Moses was also given the news that his appeal was denied.

The C.O.'s surprised me with a birthday cake. How did they know that today I was 25! Well, that just made my day. Mama and daddy surprised me with some books I had written to them about, I was so sad when they had to leave. Keith and Nell were away at college, but they sent cards and wished me well. I waited and waited but Alice never came................

Chaplain Henry was replaced by a new ministry and each week they always sent somebody different. I was told that if I wanted to get blessed that I had to tithe into their ministry. They kept reminding me that it was because of my sin that I was sentenced to prison. One day I had had enough and I told that charlatan chaplain to take me off his list and to never bother me again.

The C.O. on duty came to my cell and escorted that phony to the gate and released him into the next corridor and came back and told me that I did the right thing, and his conduct would be reported to the warden.

The next morning, I received a letter from Alice. It had been a while since I heard from her. I hurriedly tore open the letter and as I started to read, I suddenly stopped and then slowly read the first line again: "Moses, I am getting married.............."

Moses had been incarcerated for over ten years. To him that seemed like a little more than a lifetime. He had earned a Bachelor of Science degree and planned on taking courses in veterinary medicine as well as continue his law courses. Visits from family were few, far and in between. Alice was married and though she still wrote from time to time, her letters to him didn't have the same meaning. He finally stopped answering and put all his faith in God.

I was in my thirties now and gray specks started sprouting in my full beard. I was starting to look like Moses in the Bible. Due to my request for an appeal, my sixth attorney was able to keep me in my current status. I had yet to be assigned to Death Row. I was yet keeping the faith.

On Tuesday, Wednesday and Thursday I was assigned Chapel duty and was allowed to preach and teach the other inmates. I was ordained a minister by the "Second Chance At Life Church" and became a part of their ministry behind bars. I was still hoping one day to be free to resume living.

I met with the Warden for the first time, and he was impressed with all the work I was doing, and he privately agreed that I probably should never have been arrested much less convicted. He was well aware of my situation and tried to make my accommodations as comfortable as possible.

It reminds me of the story of Joseph in the Bible when he was falsely accused and imprisoned. Joseph kept the faith and received favor all the time while he was imprisoned. And after many years in prison, he was released and made the second in command to Pharoah. That was my dream from the time I set foot in that prison. Patience, Moses Aaron. Patience.......

The Warden had given Moses permission to work with the local animal shelters and soon the prison became a refuge for abused animals. Moses began to train other inmates on how to care for these animals. This gave his fellow inmates an opportunity to learn a skill and helped them to cope with their surroundings. Soon High School students were becoming part of the prison programs and were being mentored by the inmates on how to stay out of trouble and it became sort of like a big brother, little brother mentorship.

Keeping busy while in prison helped Moses as well as the other inmates keep their sanity. Moses went from being in his cell 23 hours a day when he first arrived; to having freedom to move in and around the prison. The only privilege he didn't have was the ability to leave the institution. Moses became a Doctor of Veterinary Medicine while in prison.

Being around the animals was therapy for me and the guys. The animals loved us, and we loved them. The prison staff were able to adopt pets and bring them home to their children and other family members, including themselves. Moses Aaron, like Joseph was making a name for himself behind bars.

Moses was running out of appeals. Lawyers were demanding hefty fees to process the appeals. He had already served 20 years of his death sentence. He had entered the new millennium without receiving any new news.

Abraham Aaron departed this life, suddenly and without warning. Moses watched the service several days later on a video tape provided by his baby brother Keith. Mama Aaron was too distraught to speak and was soon hospitalized after the service. They had been happily married for over forty years and had raised three children and had four grand babies.

I cried as I watched the service performed at Mt. Nebo. a church I often attended with my family. I had fond memories and I learned about both the fear and goodness of God there. Being the oldest child, I should have been the one to be there for mama. Keith's broad shoulders held mother together and kept her strong during the service. Nell provided the love and hugs that mama needed to get through the most difficult of times.

My daddy was a smart man and had recently retired debt free. He had an insurance policy that was more than adequate to provide for mama. It had already been discussed that if something ever happened to daddy that mama would go to live with Nell and her husband and children I had never met.

These are the times that were the hardest for me. I missed multiple graduations for Nell and Keith. I missed their weddings and the birth of my nieces and nephews. I could go on and on and on. If I ever wanted to escape from prison these feelings I had, only intensified my desire for my freedom.

The old Warden retired, and a new Warden took over the management of the prison and immediately made drastic changes. He ended the veterinary and animal shelter program even though it was highly successful. Next, he took away all my freedoms. I was placed back in confinement as all my previous privileges were taken away.

The next morning, Captain Crystal gave me the worst possible news that I could have ever heard next to my mother dying. All your appeals have been exhausted. Get your things together. You are being assigned to Death Row. You have been assigned to Death Block.

A numbing feeling came over me nothing but tragedy after tragedy. My mind went blank and then thoughts of Joseph flashed before me and I did what Joseph would have done, I put my trust in Almighty God.

Upon arrival on death row, I was placed in a 6' by 9' cell that was 9.5' high. I was fed 3 times a day: 5am, 11am and 4pm. I was given only a spork, (a combination plastic spoon and fork) to eat my food. I was allowed to shower on odd numbered days. I was counted every hour and was escorted in handcuffs everywhere I went. I could only leave my cell for medical issues, visits, or my exercise period. I was however allowed to receive mail and have snacks. I could watch TV and listen to the radio. I was about to begin my 20 years of famine.

I reconnected with Chaplain Henry while I was on Death Row. One day, the guard said, I have a visitor and shackled me up and took me to the visitors' area and there he was. We caught up on old times and he told me that people were on the outside still advocating for my freedom and told me to keep the faith, help is on the way.

The years went by slowly. The Governor had yet to sign off on my death decree, this gave me great hope. I did a lot of reading at this time, anything I could get my hands on. Technology was taking over the world and I was so far behind. I had never owned a cell phone or computer and I was supposed to learn to drive the summer I got arrested.

Miriam Ruth Gibbons Aaron went home to be with her husband my daddy, Abraham Aaron. It was one dark and dreary day when I got the news. I quietly sobbed as I thought about how much of her life I missed and how much of my life she missed. My mama was my rock. The moment she took her last breath, I sneezed, and I never sneezed a day, since I've been locked up in this prison.

We worked hard on the outside, trying to dig up any new evidence or witnesses that could clear Moses Aaron, an innocent man. I received a call from out of the blue from Warden Dupree who had recently retired, and he wanted to help to vindicate Moses. I immediately signed him up for the team. I never told Moses what I was doing because I didn't want to give him any false hope.

Forensic science is a critical element of the criminal justice system. Forensic scientists examine and analyze evidence from crime scenes and elsewhere to develop objective findings that can assist in the investigation and prosecution of perpetrators of crime or absolve an innocent person from suspicion.

Warden Dupree was able to have some of his contacts open a reinvestigation of the crime scene evidence and have it reexamined. He was also able to follow up with some of the witnesses. Statements were obtained from Don Wilson, Leroy Briggs and Phil Chambers that they picked up Moses at 9 pm and he was with them all night the murder took place, and they left the club together at 3 am. Moses was dropped off at about 3:30 am. Charlie Levi, admitted he gave up Moses because the cops promised if he gave them a name, they would drop the marijuana charge they busted him for. He gave up Moses because he didn't know him that well. Others witnesses interviewed indicated that they too went along for the ride.

Physical evidence was still in police custody and a DNA kit was used and the forensic team was able to obtain DNA samples from some of victims clothing. Two months after testing it was determined that Moses' DNA was not present at the crime scene. The evidence was presented in an appeal and the appeal was denied. But Moses Aaron was winning supporters and more people began to join and take a stand against false and unlawful prosecutions.

I sat on death row, 5 years….. ten years. I was 55 still waiting to die. The guards were nice though, someone baked a cake with a little candle, they had me blow it out and they sang, Happy Birthday!

The Death Warrant was issued for Moses Aaron on June 30th. Moses was moved to a Death Watch cell which is adjacent to the execution chamber. Time was running out to produce new concrete evidence to free and exonerate Moses Aaron. We had a name, Delwin Maxwell who went by the street name "King Homicide", he had been recently released from prison having completed his sentence for a murder charge, but no one knew his whereabouts.

I began to receive a lot of visitors mostly family at first, some I never ever really seen. Would you believe my first-grade teacher stopped by? And even one of the cops (now retired) needed to clear his conscience. Then, a face I didn't recognize at first, but I knew the name, Alice. Her husband had died, and she was now a widow. (I have been in this place a long time). She uttered the sweetest words that I had ever heard before she left, "I'll see you next lifetime." Chaplain Henry was one of the last to visit me and he said he heard a rumor that it was going to happen at midnight tonight. But that God does his best work at midnight.

Warden Dupree had tracked down, Delwin "King Homicide" Maxwell at a hospice and was able to obtain a signed and audio video confession. He offered details about the murder that only the killer would know. Warden Dupree had four hours to present the evidence to the Governor to get a stay of execution.

My last meal consisted of bread and wine. If I was going to be with my Savior I wanted to follow in His footsteps. To my surprise, Warden Dupree and Chaplain Henry came into the room and prayed with me. They stayed with me until the end of the execution.
The witnesses arrived and took their place. Along with the news media. I don't know how anyone can sit by and spectate somebody die.
I was given some clean garments and told to get dressed and waited in the cell for the signal that would send Moses Aaron to meet Jesus.

The evidence arrived on the Governor's desk, and he read and listened to it alone. It was a full written and video confession from "King Homicide" Delwin Maxwell. He looked at the clock it was 11:45pm

They had me lie down so they could connect an EKG machine to my body so they would know the time my heart stopped and all life as we know it had left me. I was given the option of walking on my own or being strapped to a gurney. I chose the former as I walked my Via Dolarosa. Once in the room I was tightly secured to the gurney with ankle and wrist restraints. I refused to be covered with a sheet. An IV tube was placed into each arm. The tubes were then threaded through an opening in the wall that leads to where the "executioner" is located. A saline solution was inserted and began to flow into me.

The Curtain was drawn back, and the audience were allowed to view the execution of Moses Aaron.
Moses Aaron's last words, his final statements before the lethal injection were: "*Stand still and see the salvation of the Lord which you will see today with your own eyes.*"

The Governor held the power of life and death over Moses Aaron. All he had to do was to place a call but......The clock was at 11:59.

The warden gave the signal and a deadly combination of pentothal, pavulon and potassium chloride three lethal doses were injected into the IV tube. Then they received the stay from the Governor.

The call came too late as Moses Aaron's body had already received the fatal dose. The room fell silent because an innocent man had been put to death and the man with the power to save him delivered a slow hand.

I was conscience of my spirit as I keep repeating, "I shall not die but live and declare the works of the Lord." I could feel my heart still beating, pounding, not getting weaker but stronger, stronger, and stronger. If they were waiting for Moses Aaron to die they were about to witness a miracle.

The physician assigned to pronounce death over Moses was confounded. One, two, five minutes passed and at the seven-minute mark, Moses Aaron, shouted, *"loose me and set me free!"* The doctor quickly ordered that the restraints be taken off and he was immediately examined.

Moses Aaron's initial conviction was overturned. After spending nearly 40 years in prison, the last 20 on death row he was finally free. It took several days for all the paperwork to be filed and completed but on July 6th, he walked out of prison and death row, an exonerated man. Warden Dupree, Chaplain Henry as well as family, friends and people who were part of the crusade to "Let Moses Aaron Go!" all cheered as he walked out wearing a blue suit, white shirt, and red tie.

I kissed the ground outside the prison which was off lifts to me until today and thanked everyone who stood by me through my 14,600-day campaign for freedom and then left to visit my parents' grave. I don't know how long I weep. Keith and Nell and the other family members that came with us gave me all the time I needed. I had so much to say to them and I thanked them for always believing in me. I felt a strong hand on my shoulder and a kiss on my cheek and I knew that they were celebrating with me in the 'Greater Place'.

We all went back to the house that held all my memories. A place which Keith, Nell and I called home. I went to my room and mama hadn't touched a thing, it looked like I never left. Nell and her family called the place home now and gave me carte blanche to stay as long as I wanted. I was an old man now as I looked at the pictures of a much younger me. I was fast approaching 60.

There are those of us who don't believe in God. We live life from day to day and our motto is: *"the one with the most toys wins!"* We gamble our lives away on a game of pitch and toss. But sometimes life will deal your lemons and you are unable to make lemonade. Sometimes you will be falsely accused and lied about but don't give way to lying. We are all one day going to need someone, anyone to lean on.

Why is it that when money is involved everybody suddenly wants to help? When I needed attorneys to help me litigate my case, I had no shortage of available firms at my disposal. I turned them all down and decided to use my legal skills and do it myself. I finally settled with the state for a substantial sum of money for each year I spent falsely imprisoned. But all the money in the world couldn't make up for all the years of my life that were lost, and I had missed.

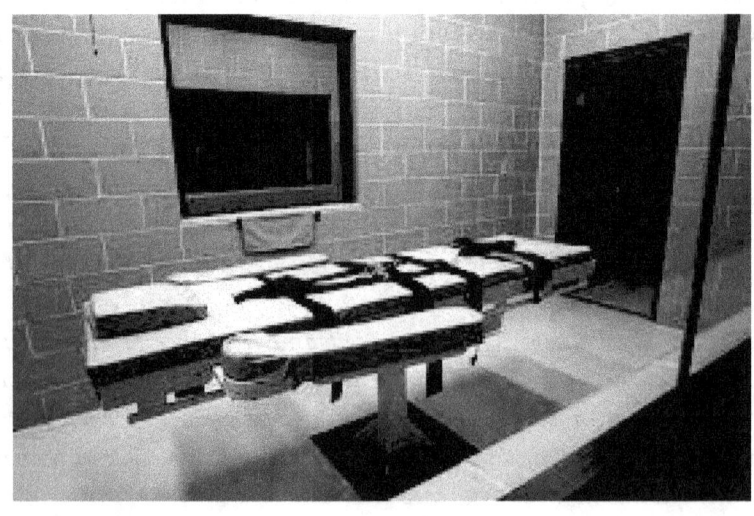

Chapter Six

"DESDEMONA"

"Kill me tomorrow; let me live tonight." (William Shakespeare)

Othello's parent named him after a character from the William Shakespeare's play of the same name. They had met and had their first date and fell in love during the second act. Othello was conceived sometimes between the third to fifth act. They were married shortly after she found out she was with child. Both parents agreed that it was the right and only thing to do.

Othello's young father had to quit school and became an apprentice and worked hard to support he and his young wife and soon to be child. The day he was born there was no doubt in their minds what they were going to name him. They both mouthed, "Othello" and the doctor said, *"then that settles it."*

Othello grew up to be a fine lad. He was good looking and well liked. He was at the top of his class in school. But most of all he was dearly loved by his mother, father and both sets of grandparents. He was an only child and reveled in his status.

After graduation, Othello settled in his career and like his parents he too fell in love at a Shakespeare play. He always referred to his young bride to be as, Lady Macbeth, Queen of Scotland. They had a fabulous wedding. Her father spared no expense for his only daughter. They were married in a church by a priest and over four hundred people were in attendance. Othello and Lady Macbeth's wedding was a lavish production. Shakespeare would have loved it.

Othello and Lady Macbeth moved into a fine home which they referred to as their little love nest. Othello had a fine career and Lady Macbeth maintained a fine home. Before long they got the news they were longing to hear. The doctor informed them that they were going to have a baby but not just one baby, twins.

The day finally came when she gave birth and into the world came two beautiful bright-eyed girls. The first one they name Viola and the second, Desdemona.

Though Othello had hoped for a boy and girl, he and Lady Macbeth were thrilled that both were born healthy. The girls gave their parents great joy and they lived as one big happy family.

Princess Vi and Princess Des as they were affectionally called were loved by all. Their maternal and paternal grandparents spoiled them rotten, and they took turns spending their summers with each one so that Othello and Lady Macbeth could have some quality alone time.

When the girls got older and began to develop personalities it became obvious that though they might be identical they were beginning to develop a lot of differences. Viola loved to play with dolls and have tea parties. Desdemona would rather play in the mud and do the craziest of things. Vi often played dress up with mommy while Des preferred to roughhouse with daddy. Vi was affectionately called her mother's joy and Des, daddy's little girl.

Vi loved to put on pretty dresses and wear ribbons in her hair while Des loved her jeans and sneakers. Vi enjoyed cooking with mommy while Des loved fishing with daddy. They were about as much alike as Patty and Cathy on the *"Patty Duke Show."*

They started school and Vi excelled in the classroom while Des made her mark in sports. Both girls were well liked by their teachers and their peers. And there was never any jealousy or animosity between them.

Othello and Lady Macbeth made sure that the girls always went to the best schools and got the best education their money could buy.

They spared no expense when it came to their two homogeneous princesses.

It was almost always easy to tell the twins apart, Vi always wore dresses and shoes while Des styled in her jeans and sneaks. They thrived on their individuality and the secrets that only two sisters could share.

The girls lived a happy care-free life, the way a child should live, growing up neither too fast nor too slow. Their parents never pressured them or tried to make them do something that made them unhappy. Othello and Lady Macbeth realized that though Viola and Desdemona were comparable they were not comparable.

One day some tough girls approached Viola and surrounded her. They started to tease her and pulled the ribbons out of hair. One of the girls started to call her names and one girl hit her and knocked her down. Carlie, a girl in Viola's class ran and found Desdemona. Desdemona took off running and comforted the three girls, she knocked the daylight out of one and tripped the other and she fell to the ground. The third girl tried to run but Des caught her and hit her so hard she saw stars. That was the first and the last time anyone messed with the Jazz sisters.

Des grabbed the girl that ran by the hair and dragged her back to where Vi was and demanded that she and the other two girls apologize. By this time one of the school deans came onto the scene to investigate. The girls smiled in unison and for the rest of the school year they became the bestest of friends and were known as the *"Fav Five."*

Des was becoming a good athlete and was soon challenging and beating all the boys in track and basketball. Vi was excellent at spelling and won the school spelling bee contest. She was also given the leading role in the annual school play.

> *You are an extraordinary people,*
> *Living in an extraordinary time,*
> *Doing extraordinary things,*
> *Written in an extraordinary rhyme.*

TARRENT-'AUTHUR' HENRY

What if I taught you,
Taught you how to multiply,
For every dollar,
I can turn it to five.

What if I coached you,
And made you the best,
If I put in the time,
So you'd pass every test.

What if I gave you,
The key to success,
Placed in your hand,
How to clean up your mess.

Are you one of those people,
That is shaking your head,
A doubting Thomas,
A drop-dead Fred.

One of those people,
That just can't believe,
A klump like Sherman or,
An urkel like Steve.

Who would you call,
To tell the good news,
If I gave you an offer,
Impossible to refuse.

Where would you go,
When would you believe,
How would you get there,
Why would you leave.

I'm an ordinary person,

Living in an ordinary time,
Doing ordinary things,
Living in an ordinary time.

The time came when Portia Jazz had to have that discussion with her two young daughters. The talk with which every mother nervously struggles; finding the right words to explain to her daughter the changes that she is about to experience in her body. Viola and Desdemona listened intently as their mother spoke to them about womanhood, she weaved her words like a ballerina dancing to a concerto.

Viola young body began to take form. Her mother took both girls shopping for items that they would need during the change, and she explained how to wear them and when to use them. Des on the only hand was slow to develop.

Three years had passed, and Viola began to fill out and go through all the sexual, physical, emotional, and psychological changes that a young girl her age goes through. Des on the other hand didn't go through any. This worried both Portia and Othello but it never seemed to bother Des.

Des went for her annual check-up with the Pediatrician, and he was also concerned because Des had not had her first period. Tests were taken and when the results came back, she was diagnosed with amenorrhea (absence of menstrual period) but other than that he gave her a clean bill of health. He reassured the family that it was nothing to worry about at the immediate time because she had a normal and healthy body.

Vi and Des began to explore their new bodies. Vi with make-up and jewelry. Des became fascinated with exercise and working out. Vi's favorite magazine was "Vogue" while Des gravitated toward "Sports Illustrated." Vi and Des also began to share intimate secrets with each other.

Vi's activities evolved around girls and doing girly things. She was in all the girl clubs at school. Des on the hand hung around boys and often outperformed them on the athletic field. The girls were growing older and beginning to find their place in the world.

Othello decided it was time for each daughter to have their own room, so he remodeled the house, and another room was added for Viola. She was the oldest, so she got the privilege to choose.

Othello was so proud of his not-so-little-anymore princesses. He watched Des grow up and taught her everything he knew and now she even outdid him in some of those things. Vi, was more domesticated and took after her mother she had a flare for cooking and decorating. But both girls made him equally proud. Vi, for her academic achievements and Des for her athletic awards.

Soon, it was time for both girls to pick and choose their colleges. Both girls wanted to leave home and see the world. Vi got her wish when she received a Fulbright Scholarship and would be leaving for Italy to start her education. Des was accepted at the University of Toronto. Both girls were excited to start their new lives. Vi and Des may have been born identical but as they grew older, they drifted farther and farther apart.

When they both left for college, Othello and Lady Macbeth would be empty nesters for the first time. They saw each young woman off separately as each left to start their college careers in a foreign country, alone and on their own for the first time in their young adult lives.

It was my first trip to Canada as I boarded Air Canada Flight 175. I was on my way to Toronto. This was a trip I needed to take to find myself and be myself. Maybe I had known for a long time, but I needed to be sure. Going away to college gave me the opportunity to discover who I really was. I was about to engage in Desdemona Jazz's coming out party.

I had always been just one of the boys. From the time I came out of my mother's womb, I guess. Did my parents sense that I was different? If they did neither ever let on, they loved me for me and isn't that all that really matters. But before I came out and told them, I wanted to be sure that it wasn't a mistake, and I was doing the right thing.

You don't know what it's like to have these feelings. I always gravitated to the boys and the things that boys do. I was also able to be just as good, fast, and strong as they were and when I got older the ones that tried to get fresh with me got what was coming to them. And big sister Vi, she never had to fight because I fought all her battles.

Vi and I use to talk about it. She was so girly, girly, and as we got older, she saw some things in me that weren't normal for a girl. Being twins, we shared the same karma and deep down inside, Vi knew what I was going through and she loved me through it.

Vi and I use to talk about boys, and she would tell me ones she was attracted to, and I would look at her and laugh because I had no feelings either way. She had often asked me, what boys I liked, seeing I was around them all the time. One day, out of the blue, I said, "You know Francine's cute!" Vi, just looked at me quite lecherously and said, "Oh, Frankie!"

Vi was the one that suggested to daddy that we have separate rooms. We both use to have these dreams at night. Vi about boys and me about girls. And the conversations we had about them always got a little weird. I hated wearing bras and all those frilly things. Vi just couldn't understand why I'd rather wear a baseball cap than comb my hair.

When daddy took me out on a date each month, after we both turned sixteen, was the only time I did my hair. Daddy was cool though, he let me wear pants if I combed my hair and didn't wear my baseball cap. On the other hand, Vi dressed up like she was going for a night out on Broadway.

I started reading books and doing on-line research about the way I was feeling. But I was afraid to reach out to any adults or share how I was really feeling and what I was going through. Then during my senior year in high school, I had an encounter with Francine.

Francine was going through some of the same things I was going through. We became confidants. We tried to focus on boys, but the topic seemed to always fall back on girls. And usually, us. Since we didn't have much experience, we never had any physical encounters We just talked and wondered why we were different.

I was handing out religious tracts and Gospels of John when two men approached me. One man got in my face and the other came behind me and asked for my wallet. He appeared to have some type of an object in his hand. I kept my cool, and my mouth shut as a person wearing a tight black leather suit and wearing a kufi burst on the scene and shouted, *"Thunder Cat – Ho!"* and those two wanna-be thieves took off running down the street.

I put my hand out to give this person a tract and Gospel of John, but they politely refused. I thanked them and introduced myself. I found out this person's name was Des. Des stood there with their spinner luggage and asked me if I knew a cheap place where there was a room available for a few nights. I got the impression that Des needed help. I didn't know why I felt that way, but I did. In my line of work, you meet all kinds of people, and my mission is to help.

I pointed Des in the direction of a place I knew that might be able to accommodate them and went about handing out tracts and spreading the good news.

Later, that evening I was conducting a meeting for wayward souls and people trying to get their lives together. As the meeting ended and I was leaving, I felt a firm hand grab my right shoulder from behind one of the pillars. I spun around and this person dressed in black leather and wearing a kufi fell into my arms and said, *"Please help me!"* It was Des.

I held Des for a very long time in silence. Des wouldn't let go and I held onto them for dear life. I decided I would let them be the first to speak. At the mission we had rooms that we made available in situations like this. This was certainly one of those situations. I gave Des all the time they needed before we went into my office. I offered Des a cup of green tea and a slice of carrot cake left over from the meeting and then Des started to tell me their story.

> *"Pastor, I don't know who or what I am anymore. I don't identify with anything or anyone. I think I'm going crazy and I'm losing my mind, what's wrong with me?"*

I asked Des, when was the last time they had gotten any sleep. They said," *I was on my way home to see my mother and father when I just flipped out and couldn't get on the plane."* Then they asked me what day it was. I said, it was Wednesday. They said, it was Thursday that they were supposed to leave. You need some sleep. Let's get you bedded down, and we'll talk in the morning. It was Friday when I got to talk to Des. We cooked Des up a good breakfast and I assigned my morning routine to one of the other ministers and we took a walk to the park and found a nice cool quiet place where we talked for hours.

Des talked and I listened, taking in every word. I usually don't minister alone in these types of situations, but I knew Des was more comfortable talking to me because we had already bonded. I was where they were at one time in my life, and I thank God for reaching out His Hand and rescuing me.

Normal can be defined as any behavior or condition which is usual, expected, typical or conforms to a pre-existing standard. 'Normal Behavior' may be defined as any behavior which conforms to social norms, which are expected or typical patterns of human behavior in any given society.

People not being themselves often leads to confusion. You can't be who someone else perceives you to be when you are not wired that way. You must function the way you were meant to function. A gasoline engine cannot run on diesel fuel. God has already wired us from birth, and he has given us an instruction manual on how to live this life called the B-I-B-L-E. Whether you believe in God or not, His laws govern the entire universe. What goes up must come down is God's law not man's. We can only predicate the weather; God creates the weather. We call it abortion; God deems it child sacrifice. There is no getting around God who created us in His image as we are creators as he is the Divine Creator, and we have intelligence as He is Divine Intelligence. What other living creature has the same attributes as man?

Tell me if you know? Can a lion build a skyscraper? No man has all the attributes of A Living Spirit God!

Des had hit rock bottom. Des wanted to go home but had gotten all mess up while away at school. Des wanted to come out of her personal closet, but Des didn't know how. Des started to hear voices in her head on how she would be perceived. Des attended church and knew God but heard it preached that her life choice was not acceptable to God. When Des went there for comfort she was cast out and literally stoned because she was wired differently. But God never turned His back on Des, the church did.

The Word of God teaches us not to judge others but to love others. We catch them and we let God clean and transform them. *There is now no condemnation to those of us who are in Christ Jesus.* We need to stop condemning and start loving. There is no sin greater than another, sin is sin. When I was struggling with my sexuality, I turned it over to Jesus and let Jesus work it out. When I struggled with finance, I turned it over to Jesus and Jesus worked it out. When I struggled with people, I turned them over to Jesus and Jesus worked them over. (Just seeing if you were paying attention} But you get my drift.

Bring all your troubles, burdens and heartaches to Jesus and Jesus will work them all out.

Des got reconnected and gave her life to Christ and the healing process began. We never lectured Des about her lesbianism. We loved on her and then we loved on her some more. Slowly she started to heal.

And through her healing she was able to help others. Today, Dez has a strong ministry that comes along side those in the LGBTQ community and just loves on them. The ministry welcomes everyone.

The only closet Des is in now is the *"prayer closet."*

It's so important to be around the right people. I was in the company of people that were not only judgmental but outright mean. They called themselves church people, but they were nothing but hypocrites. If you didn't look, feel, dress, talk and act like them, they were ready to cast you into the pits of hell. They acted like, instead of God, I had to stand before them on judgment day.

By the time I got to New York and met Pastor I was more than just churched out. I don't even remember bursting on the scene and shouting: "Thundercat - Ho!" when those guys tried to rob him. I believe God had his hand on me and led me to this person that helped me to change my life. To whom I'd be forever grateful. Now there is nothing I won't do for the gospel. And you know that church that ostracized me, they invited me to be one of their speakers for their Women's Day Conference and guess what the topic is: "Learning to Love Your New Neighbor".

God loves us despite our differences. God loves the world, each and every one of us. You may be a believer or an unbeliever. A back slider or an atheist, God still loves you. God still cares.

God is calling you
Can you hear
The Divine Sound
Of His Voice?

God is calling you
Can you smell
The Divine Fragrance
Of His Voice?

God is calling you
Can you taste
The Divine Sweetness
Of His Voice?

God is calling you
Can you touch
Th Divine Delicacy
Of His Voice?

God is calling
Can you see
The Divine Presence
Of His Voice?

God is calling
Can you feel
The Divine Movement

In His Voice?

God is calling
Can you sense
Your Divine Calling
In His Voice?

God is calling
God is calling you
Out of your comfort zone
And into the Supernatural.

The world can sometimes be a cold, cruel and dark place. It can chew you up and spit you out and then do it over and over again. Are you sinking in the quicksand, Muskie?

Does anybody hear me?
Hear my cry?
Does anybody see me?
Or my alibi?

I was walking down the street
Minding somebody else's business
When it dawned on me
Or maybe it was early evening.

Well anyway I got back to walking
Just as you started talking.

I forgot what I wanted to say
Well anyway………

Let's get back
to the Story Avenue
That's in the Bronx ain't it
Ain't it a shame………

*Living a life
without any direction
Refusing to follow
or take any correction.*

*So being a leader
is now your greatest desire
You pumped yourself up
and called your name Sire.*

*But who is going to follow
a fool and his pride?
A fool who will only lead us
to our own genocide.*

*A person without purpose
is like a fallen leaf
A murderer, a liar,
a common thief.*

*A person without a plan
is like a ship without a sail
Any plan they concoct
is so apt to fail.*

*I was walking down the street
thanking my Father in Heaven
That He's downloaded into my spirit
The Words for Chapter Seven.*

Chapter Seven

"COMMUNITY"

"A feeling of fellowship with others, as a result of sharing common attitudes, interests, and goals."

They arrived on the scene as shots rang out. "Officer, down, Officer down!", they heard on the radio. The officer managed to find safety behind the front door of his squad car as Detective Pacheco put the pedal to the metal and headed to assist her comrade in distress. Shots rang out as she managed to wedge her vehicle between the gunfire and the downed officer. Her partner helped the injured officer inside their vehicle, and they were able to remove him safely out of the line of fire.

Her day started off just like every other day at the precinct. A female police officer in a world dominated by macho cops. Detective Pacheco had served in the military and there were rumors that she served in special forces. Behind her back, she was referred to as Detective *'Cojones.'* During training, she excelled exceedingly above all the males in her class. She was often assigned to desk duty as none of the detectives wanted to work with her.

The call came into the station: ten-thirteen (officer down all units respond) everybody grabbed a partner and headed out to respond to the call. Everyone that is, except Detective Pacheco. **Enter Skylark:**

HOW TO TURN OFF YOUR BRAIN AND LISTEN TO GOD

Detective Lieutenant Percival Timothy Skylark, a 30-year veteran of the department who was also assigned to desk duty, flipped Detective Pacheco the keys to a confiscated Escalade and said, *"You wanna drive?"* She responded, *"ya darn skippy!"* and that's how they wound up on the scene.

After dropping off the wounded officer with the EMT's, Lieutenant Skylark approached the officer in command to access the situation. Apparently, a lone gunman as far as they could tell was holed up in a building, but he was tightly barricaded in, so no one had any idea whether or not he had hostages.

Skylark decided to put his 30 years of experience to the test. *"Captain, while you wait for the S.W.A.T. team do you mind if Detective Pacheco and I try something?"* He never waited for an answer as he grabbed a police force issued sniper rifle from the confiscated Escalade and handed it to the detective, *"Do you still remember how to do this, Pacheco?"* She boldly said, *"Yes. Sir!"*

"Here's the plan, I will draw his fire from over here and you will set up over there and see if you can get one good shot". *"Roger!",* she said. Within minutes, Skylark and Pacheco had put their plan into action.

Within ten minutes the crisis was over. The suspect was shot, wounded, and taken in custody by the S.W.A.T. team that had just arrived on the scene. *"You couldn't wait, Skylark. You couldn't wait."* *"No, offense, S.W.A.T. Commander but the glory doesn't belong to you, it belongs to God!"* *"I've seen your team in action and that suspect would have been dead instead of in police custody. Never underestimate an old detective and a highly competent lady D-T."*

The S.W.A.T. Commander stood there, puzzled, and confused as the suspect was brought to the EMT bus and transported to the hospital.

Skylark and Pacheco hoped in the Escalade and headed back to the station. *"Hungry?"* *"Starved,* she said, *but shouldn't we be heading back to write our reports?"* *"Detective, I think I've written enough reports for one day."* With that said, they headed to Rosalita's.

They sat down to a meal of sancocho (stew) with rice. Ana Pacheco was surprised at how much Lieutenant Skylark knew about her. *"That's my job",* he said. He decided to take her under his wings and share with her what he learned in his 30 years of experience on the force.

By the time they arrived at the precinct. The Captain and S.W.A.T. Commander had written their reports and taken full credit for the capture and arrest of the armed sniper. Skylark looked at Pacheco and said, *"the good ole boy network does it again," a*nd they both proceeded to walk back to their respective assigned cubby holes.

Chief Frank Giordano intercepted Detective Lieutenant Skylark as he headed back to his tiny cubby hole which masqueraded as an office. *"Skylark, into my office, stat!"* Once inside, he lit into Skylark like he was some rookie. Skylark stood and listened but when the chief had finished, without a word, he turned around and headed to his cubby hole where The Police Chaplain was waiting for him.

Chatroy W. Ballew has been a Chaplain for 5 years. He and the lieutenant go back a long way, they were the first two black officers to be promoted to detective sergeant in the department and had remained lifelong friends. Skylark closed the door and the two men chatted. Ballew announced that he had put in his retirement papers and was relocating to Arizona because it would help his wife's osteoporosis (a condition where bones become weak and brittle) and asked him if he would join them.

Skylark reminded Ballew of his commitment to remain on the force to mentor other minority officers and oversee more diversity in the department.

The average police force in United States 67% of the officers are White (non-Hispanic) 12.4% are Black (non-Hispanic) 11.5% are White (Hispanic) 6.1% are (Asian) 0.4% are Black (Hispanic) 2.6% are Other.

Sky-Ballew as they were called established themselves in the department by hard work and honest policing. They were respected because they were tough but fair. Even their white counterparts had to admit that they were excellent officers who they were proud to work with. As they were both reaching the end of their line, they wanted to leave a legacy that other minority officers could be proud of and build on.

Institutional racism, also known as systemic racism, is a form of racism that is embedded through laws and regulations within society or an organization. It can lead to such issues as discrimination in criminal justice, employment, housing, health care, political power, and education, among other issues.

The laws of this land were instituted by white men and the system put in place in law enforcement as well as in politics, religion and in the marketplace and even today the power still belongs to white men. Minorities have always been denied a seat at the table and in the words of Shirley Chisholm, *"if they don't give you a seat at the table, bring a folding chair."* More minority representation is needed to bring about the proper changes in the "system."

When it comes to women, they make up only 12.8% of police officers while men represent 87.2% And women earn 96% of what the average male officer earns. A seat at the table is definitely needed when it comes to bringing more women aboard. And we have not even touched base with the LGBQT community.

Skylark always maintained a resident in his old community. These streets are where he grew up and learned to sharpen his ax. Sky and Ballew lived on the same block, right next door to each other. They were two boys who chose to lead rather than follow. While some of the other young colored boys looked for trouble in the streets, Percival and Chatroy searched to find solutions.

Their parents were hard working. Chatroy's father owned a barber shop, and his mother ran a beauty salon in the back. Skylark's father was an auto mechanic and his mother worked in a hospital. The boys were always together and always full of new ideas.

Sky-Ballew found their female counterparts as young boys. Two little girls that they met who were being bullied by another group of kids. They arrived like super-heroes and rescued them from the taunts, teasing and pulling of hair and bought them each an ice cream cone. Let me let them tell the story:

"What were we Ballew, nine ten?" "Yeah, nine-an-a-half, they were surrounded by these girls and a few guys, and they were picking on our new girls on the block." "They moved in about a week apart and you know how

kids are…they were kinda sorta giving them a block initiation when it got a little out of hand." "And we sprang into action" ……. Sky cut in, *"Like two knights in shining armor."* "Adella Rodriquez, had the cutest brown eyes." ……Bellew interrupted, *"And Tiana Thikana, had this innocence in her's."* "Well, you know how boys are? We volunteered to protect them and be their chaperones." Sky added, *"and the rest is history, it's in the book."* "We ended up marrying those two girls, Thik and Rod."

    The next story you are about to read is going to blow you away. Please read slowly and pay close attention. Sky-Ballew and Thik-Rod loved to explore, investigate, and examine things. One day they were walking from the pizza shop and as they walked past, The Golden Dragon, they heard several men speaking or rather arguing in Chinese. The men wound up in the street wielding weapons. The children ran to a nearby building where they ducked so they couldn't be seen. One of the Asian men struck what appeared to be an old white haired Chinese man with a green bladed sword. The old man fell to the ground and the other men quickly fled.

    Sky-Ballew and Thik-Rod were scared but curious, suppose the man needed help?

    They decided the coast was clear and ran over to investigate. When they got close enough to examine the sidewalk, the man's body had instantly disappeared. They were momentarily startled but still mustered up the courage to check out the scene. There was no body, no blood and The Golden Dragon was filled with people sitting and eating. They were even bold enough to tell some of the people in the Chinese restaurant what they witnessed but they laughed them off as day-dreaming kids.

    They knew they saw an old white haired Chinese man struck to the grown with a sword. And thus, this youthful foursome had their first big case as gumshoe detectives. It wasn't until many years later when Sky and Ballew became detectives and Rod became an attorney and Thik, a coroner in the medical examiner's office that the mystery would be solved.

    The Golden Dragon caught on fire and nearly burned to the ground. After every fire there is an investigation and during the one for the Chinese restaurant a decaying body was found in a hidden cellar below the basement. The body was brought to the medical examiner and assigned to Thik to determine cause and time of death. She determined that the man had been dead for about thirty years and his cause of death was blunt trauma force. She immediately called her husband.

The case of the Chinese man and the only witnesses were four young children who were told that they must have been daydreaming. Detective Sergeant Percival Timothy Skylark and Detective Sergeant Chatroy W. Ballew were assigned to the case of the dead unidentified old white haired Chinese man who cause of death was listed as possible homicide.

The first thing they did was try to establish his identity, DNA, fingerprints and dental records didn't yield any results, so they searched through missing person records from around the time of his disappearance and death. They found a name that matched his description. Li Wong Chang's family had reported him missing around the same time that the murder had taken place.

The Chang family was contacted and some of the family remembered him. Lee, as he was called was carrying a family secret that apparently, he took to his death, and it was the detectives' job to bring the people responsible for his murder to justice.

> *Got to keep on walking,*
> *Walking through the park,*
> *Got to keep on walking,*
> *Percival Timothy Skylark.*
>
> *Got to keep on searching,*
> *Searching for the clue,*
> *Got to keep on searching,*
> *Chatroy Willson Ballew.*
>
> *Every bodies talking,*
> *The chicks keep on squawking,*
> *There's no two ways about it,*
> *The dudes they allowed it.*

The Chinese man,
When he needed a friend
There was none around,
So his life came to an end.

The man had a secret,
He wasn't willing to share,
The secret that Tiana Thikana
Found in a lock of his hair.

So Percival Timothy Skylark,
And Attorney Adella Rod
Gave Chatroy Willson Ballew,
And Tiana Thikana the nod.

The Chinese man's secret was found in a lock of hair that miraculously survived all those years as the body decomposed and that secret was about to lead our detectives to who was responsible for the old man's death.

Detective Pacheco sat in her chair in her cubicle handling dispatch when several detectives came over and said, *"Pacheco, you really handled yourself today. We just want to be the first to congratulate you on a job well done. Hoskins is in the hospital, and he told us all how you saved his bacon and we just wanted to invite you out with us this evening."* Ana Pacheco, sat up straight in her chair, it took her about thirty seconds to react, *"Sure,* she said, *what time?"*

Sometimes you just have to do it,
Roll up your sleeves,
Lift your arms and do it.

You have to be the one,
To get out of your comfort zone,
Take a stand and do it.

HOW TO TURN OFF YOUR BRAIN AND LISTEN TO GOD

Everyone has got their eyes on you,
Are you going to flee?
Or are you going to fight?

Now is not the time,
To back down,
Rise up and take it.

Get out of,
That comfort zone,
And make it.

Everyone has got their eyes on you,
Are you going to flee?
Or are you going to fight?

You've run out of excuses,
Treys are running wild,
Not duces.

Don't be scared,
Just be prepared,
And do it.

Everyone has got their eyes on you,
Are you going to flee?

Or are you going to fight?

Chapter Eight

"RSL"

(Reasons – Seasons – Lifetime)

In this chapter we are going to talk about relationship and why people come into your life. If we know why then we can begin to develop an understanding and save ourselves unnecessary pain when the relationship does a full 360 on us. Follow along with me as we visit:

Reasons

Matilda recently met Susan at the supermarket. The two women chatted in line while both were waiting to pay for their groceries. When Susan's turn came to pay, she couldn't find her wallet. Since it was only a few items, Matilda offered to pay for the groceries on her credit card and Susan could pay her later. Susan gave Matilda her cell number and said she would call her and the two could meet for lunch later in the week and she would give her the money that she owed. One day, then two days went by, and Matilda decided to call Susan and as would have it, the number just rang and rang. Matilda later realized that Susan had given her a fake number.

There are people who want to reach out to you for a reason unbeknownst to you. What appears to be an attempt to strike up an immediate friendship often turns into a con job. These can be a onetime encounter like Matilda and Susan or one like this:

Daniel started a new job in a hospital. He was a nice guy, friendly and always ready to lend a helping hand. On the first day on the job, he met Felix who worked in another department and the two would chat it up from time to time. After knowing each other for several weeks. Felix hit Daniel up for $20.00 and promised to pay him back on pay day. Pay day came and Felix said, he was a little short and offered to give Daniel $10.00. Daniel accepted and Felix promised to pay on his next pay day. Two days before pay day, Felix paid Daniel back the other $10.00.

Another week went by, and Felix asked Daniel for a big favor, he needed to borrow money again. This time $30.00. Since Felix paid Daniel back the $20.00, he saw no reason not to trust Felix. After all they were friends, pals, and co-workers. Two weeks went by, and Daniel never saw Felix. He asked around and learned Felix was coming to work but had been avoiding him. Another co-worker informed Daniel that Felix was notorious for setting people up by borrowing money with no intentions of ever paying them back.

Maybe you're like Daniel and have a co-worker that wants to be your friend for a reason. These 'Reason Friends' are smooth operators. They pick who they want to manipulate carefully. Here are some signs to look for so your name doesn't fall on their list:

- Beware of the skilled liar.
- Beware of those that don't follow through on their actions.
- Beware of those who try to put you on a guilt trip.
- Beware of those who play the victim role.
- Beware of those who share too much personal information.
- Beware of emotional manipulators.
- Beware of someone who is always eager to help.
- Beware of someone who tells amazing stories.
- Beware of someone who knows too much about you.

Somebody who talks about everybody talks about you too. Some call it their intuition. Some discernment. One is from man. One is from God. Choose discernment because God is never wrong. As we learn to listen to God, he downloads information into us and opens our eyes so we can see the true nature of our new acquaintances. Is this someone I should help or is this someone who is out to hurt me?

There are four basic personality types:
(Using Peanut Characters as an illustration)

- Type A – Likes to be in control. (Lucy)
- Type B – Likes to be the center of attention. (Snoopy)
- Type C – Detail-oriented (Linus)
- Type D – Routine – (Charlie Brown)
- Type X – Combination of A B C D – (Shroeder)

It is important to keep your guard up when it comes to identifying whom you allow access into your life. What can start off like a request for conversation can become a pry into your life. Case in point:

I was waiting in an airport terminal to take a flight to attend a funeral. The flight was delayed so all the passengers were getting a little antsy. A gentleman started a conversation with me that seemed simple at first and then he began to pry into my personal life and immediately my antenna went up. He was using the fact that I told him why and where I was going as an opportunity to pry personal information out of me. Well, I stood up, raised my voice and I let him know that I did not appreciate where our conversation was going and suggested he take himself and his carrying on luggage to another waiting area. My actions must have caught the attention of all the people in the waiting area. The man now embarrassed without another word quickly wheeled he and his bag out of the terminal. Turns out he wasn't even on the same flight I was on; he was looking to befriend me for a wrong reason. *'Beware of the handshake that hides the snake.'*

Earl had broken up with his wife and needed a place to stay so he called his friend Steve. Steve had an extra room and told Earl that he could come over and stay the night. When Steve got up to go to work the next morning, Earl decided to take a sick day because he was tired and worn out from the argument he had with his wife from the night before. Steve left him the spare key and told Earl he would see him after work, and they would talk.

Steve arrived back home from work and saw Earl lying on the couch with his feet propped up, watching TV with food and beer spread out over the table. He pretended not to notice as he walked back to his bedroom. He noticed that Earl had already moved some of his stuff in the spare room.

This went on for two weeks until Steve confronted Earl about their living arrangement. He explained to Earl that he was just being a good friend by letting him stay the night but had not expected him to move himself in and make himself at home like it was his apartment. Steve said, he was sorry about the state of his marriage, but the living arrangement had to end.

Earl lit into Steve and Steve reminded Earl of all the times when he got in a jam that he used his kindness to take advantage of him and it was stopping today. He informed Earl that he could stay the night and he would help him find another place in the morning. Earl then hit Steve and the two men began to tussle. A neighbor who overheard them arguing called the police and they soon arrived and Earl was arrested.

When I look back on the incident, said Steve, I don't know why I let someone like Earl manipulate me. He had a bad habit of making his problem, my problem. The best thing that ever happened to me was that fight because it opened my eyes. Earl kept me as a friend for a reason, his selfish reason. There was never any real friendship between us. Anytime, he needed money, an alibi or a place to stay he always called me.

This relationship is the classic example of a *"Reason Relationship."* 'Don't allow an Earl's handshake or smile to fool you. Take my advice, I'm only trying to school ya.' Someone like Earl will only keep you around as a friend so they can use and re-use you like a book end. Take a moment, to examine your friendships. Are there any Earl or Earline's that you need to remove?

Suddenly, you came into my life,

And you quickly took it over.
Instead of asking me,
You told me what to do.

What was mine,
Was now yours.
Today, I'm turning the tables,
I'm flipping the script.

Now find the exit.

We now go from reasons to:

Seasons

On Earth, a Season is a period of the year distinguished by special climate changes. There are four seasons, spring, summer, fall (autumn) and winter. Relationships also have seasons. When we think of seasons and relationships, we usually acquaint them as plutonic. But did you know that there are seasons in every relationship?

New relationships start in Spring. During this season, we get to know each other. This is the season where chemistry is developed. Summer is where things get hot in the relationship, where best friend bonds develop. Fall or Autumn is where we start to see the relationship for what it really is, our connections are put into boxes and labeled. Winter is when the relationship waxes cold, and communication becomes non-existent.

Sasha and Terri were in their first semester in college and as they waited in line to turn in their financial aid forms, they struck up a conversation and discovered that they had a lot in common. They continued their conversation after turning the forms in and since they were hungry decided to go to the cafeteria to grab a bite to eat. They found out that they both lived in the same state but different cities and decided after lunch to go see the Residence Hall Director to inquire if they could be roommates. They remained roommates for all four years at the university and were known as the *"Bobbsey Twins"* on campus because where Sasha went, Terri was never too far behind. This is an example of a Spring relationship that blossomed into Summer.

Oscar and Rob played together on the same team. Oscar was the starter and Rob rode the bench. Oscar got hurt in the game and Rob subbed in. The trainer told Oscar that he would have to miss several games. The coach inserted Rob into the starting lineup. Oscar and Rob were close pals both on and off the court before the injury. They even rooted for each other in the game. But it soon became apparent that Rob was playing better that Oscar. The coach indicated that Rob was going to stay in the starting line-up. Soon, Oscar found it hard to cheer for Rob on the bench. His wish was for him to get injured so he could get back his starting job. He began to spend less and less time with Rob. Their relationship soon grew apart until they barely acknowledged each other, and it went from a Fall relationship into a cold Winter one.

I am going to ask you now. Examine your relationships. Who are you in a Spring relationship with? Summer? Fall? Winter? Which relationships are keepers? Which are weepers? What relationships need to be nurtured? What relationships need to be pruned? What relationships have to end? Who in your relationships are for you? Who are against you? Take your time to complete this assignment.

Statistics say that the average American has three friends for life. Five people they like and spend time with and eight people they like and don't spend time with. *'The truth is in the eye because the eye don't lie, Amen'.* How many people can you look in the eye and say, friend?

In this new age of technology, face-to-face meetings have been replaced by text messages and zoom meetings. We spend so much time on our Smart-Phones that we are treating them like best friends or family. We don't take the time to nurture our relationships. People just drift in and out of the seasons in our lives.

Drifting on a sea of forgetfulness trying to sail home. But where is home?

Home is a place where you use to live but now you don't live there anymore.

As you walk in and out and through the four seasons of your life. Do you have any regrets?

Some of us are longing for friendships that we shared from back in the day. Memories?

Trying to live in the past but everything must change. Secrets must be revealed.

I am writing this from a place of strength, and I thank God for creating seasons.

Lord, I just want to say thank you for my life and all those that you lead to read the words that you have downloaded into me to share with your people. I am honored that you have chosen to use this broken vessel to send a message of love to your people. A message to let your people know that you are alive and working in our lives collectively and individually. A message that says, hold on, just a little while longer. Hold on, help is on the way.

Whatever season you are in your life. Spring-Summer-Winter or Fall, all you have to do is *"turn off your brain and call on God"*

There are seasons in life and seasons in relationships. I have just stopped by to remind you of that, and don't you forget to take a look in the mirror at your friend who is staring back at you. And sometimes our one and only friend is the reflection you will see in that mirror. I challenge you today to examine that friend in the mirror and make sure that it is the spitting image of the person you are striving to be, not a facsimile but the real you with a heart of flesh and not one of stone. One that's wearing a smile and not a frown.

In order to have a friend you must first be a friend. In your lifetime you will experience many seasons. The majority of your friendships you have will only be for a season. Friends we had as kids will end. School friends will end. Job friends will end. Friends of friends will end. Group friends will end. Sports friends will end.

We must learn where we are in the seasons. We must know when the right time is to move on and let go. Sometimes we try to hold on to a friendship when it becomes apparent that the other person is in winter. We must learn to cherish the relationship in spring and summer and be prepared to move on in autumn and winter. And always be thankful for what the friendship means to you and don't become upset if the season ends earlier than you expected.

Seasons are a time to grow. A time to learn A time to share. But when change comes remember:

- Guard your emotions.
- Never assume it's your fault.
- Pray the best for your friend.
- Believe God to send a new friend.
- Thank God for your present friend.

Start
Playing
Running
Imagination
Nurturing
Growing

Sharing
Umbrella
Munching
Mangoes
Exercise
Racing

Fading
Abandon
Lack
Lost

Was
Idle
Nobody
Traitor
Ego
Rejected

Thank you, God, for creating four seasons.
Thank you, God, for giving us reasons.
Thank you, God, for creating Eve.
Thank you, God, for her creative seed.
Thank you, God, for creating friends,
Some for now and some for then.
Thank you, God.

Thank you, God, for giving me,
As far as the naked eye can see.
Thank you, God, for every human,
And Presidents like Harry Truman.
Thank you, God for Holy Dove,
And teaching mankind how to love.
Thank you, God.

From Reasons to Seasons to:

Lifetime

Abigail and Cathy sat around drinking coffee and going over old times. They made it a habit to meet in some way shape or form at least once a month to catch up on old times. Though both now in their mid-seventies and living in different cities they still find time to keep acquaintance.

They met as young girls in elementary school as classmates and quickly found that they had a lot of things in common. And they have remained friends ever since through both the good and the bad times.

They attended the same middle school, high school and even went to the same college. Along the way they developed a bond and loved each other better than sisters. They shared many secrets along with all the highs and lows that come with life.

Abigail and Cathy supported each other and though there were fights and disagreements, the girls always managed to patch things up and remain the bestest of friends. Others even tried to break them apart, but the girls valued each other too much to let that happen.

Abigail was a bridesmaid in Cathy's wedding and even caught the bouquet. Cathy served as the maid-of-honor in Abigail's. And even though Cathy moved away when she got married, they still found time to get together along with their families to maintain their friendship.

Through, marriage, raising kids, graduations, tragedies and even death. Abigail and Cathy were always there for each other. Like marriage our friendship vow is: *"to death do we part,"* they would always say.

I asked Abigail, what was the key to a friendship that lasts a lifetime: *"Well, first off, you have to want a friend. I was raised to value myself and treat people the way I wanted to be treated. This old girl and I just connected from the first day we met. She is always and still is as sweet as molasses. We never competed with one another, as a matter of fact, we were each other's biggest supporter. And we were always there to dry each other tears and to celebrate when that was what was needed. There were times in my life when I know I couldn't have made it without Cathy's sistership and love."*

Cathy it's your turn? *"Who, are you calling old girl? (laugh) Abigail Penny Laine! If there were two girls that better complimented each other than Abby and me, I've had yet to meet them. Let me let you in on a little secret? The reason that we remained so close for so long is because we loved God and we loved each other. The first time we met, we had both been praying for a forever friend and God answered us and blessed us in ways we could never ever imagined. We both put God first and foremost in our lives and through thick and thin He was always there to guide us."*

The time came for Abigail and Cathy to say their good-byes. Cathy's grandson had arrived to pick her up and take her back home. The young girls in spirit said their last goodbyes and Cathy promised to call as soon as she reached home. There are friends for Reasons. Seasons. Lifetimes. If you had your choice which, would you choose?

In this time of Pandemic and social distancing. I don't like the term rather we should call it physical distancing. We need each other and it is especially evident in this season of COVID. Human beings were created to be tribal. We are social beings. We need each other. We were destined to operate as a group collective. We were destined to be creative and loving people and to work together for the same purposes. The human body is wired to have a sense of belonging and to feel appreciated, respected and cared for. We were designed to live together in harmony, with civility, respect, and empathy toward one another.

We must develop healthy core values such as:

- Loyalty
- Honesty
- Trust
- Ingenuity
- Accountability
- Family
- Security
- Intelligence
- Connection
- Humanity
- Success
- Diversity
- Generosity
- Integrity
- Openness
- Spirituality
- Forgiveness
- Faith
- Kindness

HOW TO TURN OFF YOUR BRAIN AND LISTEN TO GOD

- Teamwork
- Communication
- Excellence
- Commonality
- Strength
- Cooperation
- Friendship
- Relationship
- Humor
- Grace
- Compassion

>There are many types of ships,
>
>Aircraft Carrier and Battleship
>
>Clipper and Dow,
>
>East Indiaman and Frigate,
>
>Galleon and Hammer,
>
>Ironclad and Junk,
>
>Karve and Liner,
>
>Merchant and Nef,
>
>Ocean and Pram,
>
>Q and Royal,
>
>Slave and Troop,
>
>U and Victory,

Whale and Xebec,

Yacht and zee.

Although I've been a captain,

And sailed the modern seven seas,

The Arctic and The Antarctic,

North and South Atlantic,

South and North Pacific,

The Indian Ocean.

Although I've sailed on many ships,
I found friendship to be the greatest ship.

Our lives are built on relationships and friendships that last in periods of reasons, seasons, and lifetimes. People will weave in and out of your life from the time you are born until the time you die.

These relationships and friendships will all leave their mark on you. Some may even shape you or scar you for life. Before I end this chapter, I would like to leave you with some thoughts.

What kind of friend are you? Do you add value to the lives of others? Or are you subtracting?

Maybe before we choose our friends, we should conduct an interview and do a background check, a credit check, a criminal check, and a sanity test. Ask them a few questions like, do you like snakes, why or why not? What are your thoughts on cactus? Have you ever met anyone like me before?

Relationships are built one at a time, one step at a time. Relationships are built by two people wanting to have a mutual connection. Relationships are built by asking the right questions and giving truthful answers. Relationships are built by telling another person about yourself and being transparent. Relationship is about going to the same places and enjoying doing the same things.

Relationship is about accepting other people for who they are and not trying to change them.

Friendship starts when the other person wants to have a relationship with you. Friendship starts when you are over the feeling of being rejected. Friendship starts when you want to be a part of something greater than yourself. Friendship starts when I becomes, we and we becomes us.

Friendship happens when you learn to enjoy the other person and begin to value them.

So, now it's time for you to being to evaluate your friendships and relationships. And put them in the proper box. You have three boxes:

Which ones go in your reasons box?
Which belong in seasons?
And who are the friends you cherish for a lifetime?

Two of those boxes will change from time to time but that third box should withstand the tests of time.

An ancient book which we all should be familiar with says this about friends:

- A true friend loves at all times.
- A true friend sticks close than a sibling.
- A true friend is willing to lay down their life.
- A true friend intercedes for one another.
- A true friend is a blessing.
- A true friend is sweet.
- A true friend walks together in unity.
- A true friend is an encourager.
- A true friend will honor you.
- A true friend forgives.
- A true friend doesn't gossip
- A true friend lends a helping hand.

- A true friend is kind.
- A true friend will carry your burdens.
- A true friend is giving.
- A true friend is a gift from God.

Chapter Nine

"FLIGHT"
(Find-Life-In-God-Here-Today)

Nicholas Herman lived in France in the 17th century born into a life of poverty he later joined the army where he was guaranteed meals and a small salary. Upon retirement from the army, he entered the Discalced Carmelite monastery in Paris where he became as who we most commonly know him, Brother Lawrence.

Brother Lawrence was assigned to the kitchen where he developed his rule of spirituality and work. It was here where Brother Lawrence learned to give everything to God. Brother Lawrence learned the art of how to retreat to the secret place in his heart and find the love of God hidden there in all its richness and glory. He learned and taught us that even an ordinary man during the course of his ordinary work can practice and experience the presence of God. Thus, the name of his book, *("The Practice of the Presence of God")* his teachings, letters, and conversations with God.

Brother Lawrence learned to discipline his heart and mind to yield to God's presence. He was able to retreat to a place in his heart where God's love made even the simplest detail of his life of great value. He began to live as if there was only, He and God in the world. God came along side Brother Lawrence as he cooked, ran errands, and went about his daily duties.

In his book "The Practice of the Presence of God" we learn several truths:

- Our attitude in our daily activities can help to shape our character.
- Our spiritual life is essential to our environment.
- Our work should be unto God and not unto self.
- Our simple and consistent practices help to merge our work with our faith.

Brother Lawrence did his daily work for the love of God. He recognized that God wasn't only in the chapel but in the kitchen. He learned he could not hide from the presence of God. Every activity that we do is God designed to draw us closer to Him. In the 21st century we often find it difficult to keep ourselves focused on doing our work for God because of so many distractions. We often set our goals on the things of this world instead of keeping our focus on treasures in Heaven. Please take 5 seconds, put down the book, and begin to thank God. Begin to integrate God into the fabric of your life.

Brother Lawrence of the Resurrection an obscure monk from the 17th century provided us with a legacy that has lasted well over three hundred years. Every person has the ability, by the grace of God, to enjoy an ongoing fellowship with Creator God wherever he is and whatever he does.

Sunday January 1st

Reading, the Holy Bible, God's written word, from cover to cover, again and again. When I read His Word, my eyes are enlightened according to His richness in glory, and I receive new understanding. It is as if I am reading His Words for the first time.

The Word of God is alive and is sharper than any two-edged sword. The Word is Spirt and Life. Oh, how I love to taste each Word. Chew each syllable and swallow the Word Alive.

Oh, God thank you for Your sweet inspiration. It's all about You Jesus. Your Word is my guide to the blessed life.

The prophets of old did not have this entire Book. They did not have the Old and New Testament. All that had to live on was faith. The faith in a Living God.

You gave them the Words, Father. You taught them what they needed to know so they could write this Book that teaches us all how to live.

Monday January 2nd

Today is the first day of the best years of your life. Your life is about to change starting today for the better. You are about to be transformed into the image of the Living God.

Put your pass behind you, confess your sins and lay them down at the altar. Leave them all at the cross. Begin to renew your mind daily by taking in new information. Let the Holy Spirit into your heart and allow Him access so He can begin to straighten out your life.

Praise God! Hallelujah! Lift up Holy hands and with a loud voice, honor Him with your praise offering. Clap your hands and give God the glory. Thanking God for what He has already done and what He is doing. And proclaim and thank Him for all the stuff He is about to do.

Jesus is our Life. He is our Salvation. Jesus is our Source. He is our Substitute. He died so that you and I might live.

Honor Him each and every day.

Tuesday January 3rd

I give myself away to you, Lord. I give you, my life; have your way with me Lord. Shape me and remake me into the man that you want me to be. Let me have a closer walk with You Father.

My life up to this point has been cold and empty. Teach me how to love again Father God? Create in me a new and clean heart so I can begin to love others the way that you love me. Thank You, Jesus.

I am ready Lord. I am steadfast in my spirit, body, and soul to exercise my will to conform to yours. It is no longer about me, but it is all about you, Father God.

But Lord, I need Your help. I need You so desperately in my life. Please move into my body and remove any iniquity so I can be more like You.

Today is a day of new beginnings so I purpose to live my life, more and more as I am being transformed into Your image and likeness. Oh God, You haven't failed me yet.

Wednesday January 4th

We must learn to apply Your Word in every area of our lives. We are living stones and we are being transformed into Your Likeness, daily.

Oh Father God, oh how we need You more and more each day. Lord, we are so desperate for You. You are our Bread and our Wine. We are nothing apart from You.

Thank You Father for each and every blessing. Your Blessings are new each and every day. We thank You for keeping us humble. We thank You for Your Peace which You have placed within our hearts.

We thank You for Your unspeakable joy that You have spoken over our lives. You are the great and mighty Jehovah God.

Lord, You are our Daily Bread. You sustain us by Your written Word. Your Word is Alive and sharper than any two-edged sword. Teach us how to use Your Word that we might learn to live.

Thursday January 5th

Thank You Lord for all You've done for me. Oh God, You are so good.

This morning I am filled with Your omnipotent presence. My life is totally surrendered to Your will and Your ways, Hallelujah!

We have entered a new year, but Your promises remain the same. Our hearts are steadfast and focused on You.

The air that we breathe, the water that we drink. The ground that we walk on. All these things are good gifts that come from above.

Greatness is one of Your attributes, Father God. Lovingkindness and tender mercies are not too far behind.

Lord, we love You and we thank You for delivering us and keeping us each and every day.

We thank You that we have a Father that loves us unconditionally. We thank You that You have made a future home for each of us in the Heavenlies where we can all dwell with You, forever,

Friday January 6th

You are an Excellent Lord. Excellent in all Your ways. Oh God, all Your ways are past knowing. All the things that You did, have done and are still doing are written in Your Book of Life.

We honor You each day by presenting our bodies as living sacrifices, Holy and acceptable unto You. Your great compassion restrains us. Thank You, Jesus.

We rejoice and we sing, Holy, Holy, Holy! What an honor it is to be in Your Presence. Oh, how we love You, King Jesus! We lift up our hands because we are in awe of You, Thank You, Jesus.

Holy Spirit, we need You to teach us and to guide us into all truth. We need to hear a fresh Word from You each and every day. With each day comes new meaning and new revelations. Glory to Your Name!

Saturday January 7th

Sometimes Father God, I don't know where to turn. I don't know who to trust. I am lost without Your G-P-S. The world has nothing to offer me. My family and friends have deserted me. I am in a dark and desolate place.

Shine Your Light on me Lord Jesus. Let me look into the radiance of Your Glory. Heal my heart and cleanse my mind, quickly. Dry every tear and remove every sinful stain from my past. My focus today is on the Cross and the Blood.

The Cross came with a price. The cost of my sin. Your precious Blood paid that price in full. So now I am free from a life of bondage. I am free to obtain the gift that Your great sacrifice provided. The Gift of Eternal Life with You, Lord Jesus, in Glory.

Thank You, Father for opening my heart today to remind me that I have a place to turn.

Sunday January 8th

Oh God, what part of my life do You not understand?
I was created and shaped in sin. I was lost until You found me. Like a Potter You began to re-shape me.

A little here and a little there until I became Your Masterpiece. I became the object of Your Affection.

Now each morning when I awaken to fellowship with You, I am being transformed more and more into Your Image and Likeness. Oh Hallelujah, Glory to God! I am being changed into Your very image. I look like Jesus.

Oh God, I am beginning to walk like You walked. My speech incorruptible. I can do all things that You did when You were flesh and man. Now I fully understand more and more about You. Thank You for saving my life.

Watchman Nee was born in the 20th century and lived in China. Born Ni Tuo sheng he was a Chinese church leader and Christian teacher. He traveled throughout China establishing churches and held conferences to train Bible students and church workers.

Nee's own words: *"On the evening of 28th of April 1920, I was alone in my room, struggling to decide whether or not to believe in the Lord. At first, I was reluctant but as I tried to pray, I saw the magnitude of my sins and the reality and efficacy of Jesus as Savior. As I visualized the Lord's hands stretched out on the cross, they seemed to be welcoming me, and the Lord saying, 'I am here waiting to receive you.' Realizing the effectiveness of Christ's blood in cleansing my sins and being overwhelmed by such love, I accepted him there. Previously I had laughed at people who had accepted Jesus, but that evening the experience became real for me and I wept and confessed my sins, seeking the Lord's forgiveness. As I made my first prayer, I knew joy and peace such as I have never known before. Light seemed to flood the room and I said to the lord, oh, Lord, you have indeed been gracious to me."*

Watchman Nee ministered throughout China and at the age of 21 established his first local church in Malaysia. In 1928 he published a three-volume book called: *"The Spiritual Man."* The book teaches that man is a tripartite creation. God created man as a spirit, and he lives in a body and has a soul.

God showed him in the spirit what kind of work he wanted him to do:

- Written teachings.
- Church Meetings.
- Building up the local church.
- Training of youth.

Watchmen Nee ministered throughout China during World War Two and into 1949 when the Chinese Communist Party took control of the government. It was during this period that Christians in China began to come under persecution. Christians were rounded up and placed in labor camps if they refused to denounce their belief in Jesus Christ.

He was arrested in 1952 and was sentenced to fifteen years in prison under the worst type of conditions. The only visitor allowed was his wife Charity Chang. In 1971 his wife died, and he was not allowed to attend her funeral. Charity's eldest sister took over her responsibilities to care for him. Nee was scheduled to have been released from prison in 1967 but he died there in 1972 in a labor camp. There was no announcement of his death not even a funeral. His remains were cremated before his family had a chance to arrive at the prison.

Before his death, Watchman Nee left a piece of paper under his pillow which read: **"CHRIST IS THE SON OF GOD WHO DIED FOR THE REDEMPTION OF SINNERS AND RESURRECTED AFTER THREE DAYS. THIS IS THE GREATEST TRUTH IN THE UNIVERSE. I DIE BECAUSE OF MY BELIEF IN CHRIST. WATCHMAN NEE"**

Monday October 1st

Lord, have mercy on me a sinner and hear my plea. Grant me justice on today. Give me mercy for I am a sinful man born in iniquity; that was until I heard about a Man named Jesus, who is the Son of the Living God.

Jesus, Jesus, Jesus! Oh, how I love to hear that name, Jesus. I read His Story and I learned that He died so that I might live. He exchanged His sinless life for my sinful one. Jesus died for me on the tree at Calvary.

The Cross and the Blood. Justified and redeemed. Sanctified and glorified. By grace I have been saved through faith. Joy and thanksgiving flow from my heart. I am the righteousness of God.

Holy Spirit was sent to dwell inside of me, my life is now completely filled with all His Fulness.

Tuesday October 2nd

We would love to think that because we love God that all things will automatically become good, and change will immediately come upon our lives. We think that all hardships and difficulties will suddenly disappear. We expect great change expediently.

Oh God, we cry out to you this morning to have extreme mercy on us when things don't go the way we planned them. Your ways are much higher than our ways and Your thoughts our thoughts.

There is much we do not understand about Kingdom Business and righteousness. We must learn to draw nigh to you so you can draw nigh to us.

Father, we want things to happen instantly and when they don't, we feel that you have somehow abandoned us. It is at these times that we come to love you even more and experience Jesus like never before.

October 3rd

One thing that I desire of the Lord. One thing that I ask for, that I may come into His Presence and behold His lovely face and to lay at His feet and glory in the splendor and beauty of His Divine Holiness.

Lord, to be with you, to be able to inquire in Your Temple. Oh God, take me to Heaven that I may have a glimpse of where I will be present with You on the last day.

Father, forgive me for all the times I took You for granted. All the times when I made myself god. The times where I stood in the place where Christ now rules in my heart.

Lord, You have given me Your Perfect Peace. You have given me Joy unspeakable, you have put Light into my belly and become the Candle in my spirit which burns forever.

October 4th

Know your God. Learn all there is to know about Him. Be teachable. Sit at His feet and learn from Him. Honor God by presenting your body as a living sacrifice, ready to be burnt at the altar. You must be willing to be crucified with Christ so that You may become one with Him.

Lord, I rededicate my life to You this morning. Not just my heart. Not just my soul. But all of me. I give myself away to You Lord Jesus.

The day has come when we worship the Father in Spirit and in Truth. There is no other way. We place no other gods before us. We vow to live a chaste but simple life.

Empower us Lord with Your omnipotence. Give us wisdom to discern righteousness and truth. We want to know You God. Teach us today.

October 5th

It is the Lord's doing. Every woman and every man must bow down and worship the Lord. The sooner that we come to the realization that we can do nothing apart from God, the easier it will be for us to accept Jesus Christ as both Lord and Savior.

Oh God, we give ourselves away to You today. Even right now our eyes are on You and our ears are attentive to Your every Word.

Yes Lord, we love You on today and we have come to the knowledge of the beauty and splendor of Your Holiness.

Oh Lord, You are our God and we will give our lives to You in return for your fresh Anointing. The promise of Holy Spirit has been poured out on each of our lives. We have been filled with all wisdom and power.

Lord, we thank You for doing for us as You said in Your Holy Word.

October 6th

Jesus have mercy on me! Jesus have mercy on me! Jesus have mercy on me! Jesus have mercy on me!

Jesus have mercy on me! Jesus have mercy on me! Jesus have mercy on me! Jesus have mercy on me!

Jesus have mercy on me! Jesus have mercy on me! Jesus have mercy on me! Jesus have mercy on me! Jesus have mercy on me! Jesus have mercy on me! Jesus have mercy on me! Jesus have mercy on me! Jesus have mercy on me! Jesus have mercy on me! Jesus have mercy on me!

Jesus have mercy on me! Jesus have mercy on me! Jesus have mercy on me! Jesus have mercy on me!

Jesus have mercy on me! Jesus have mercy on me! Jesus have mercy on me! Jesus have mercy on me! Jesus have mercy on me! Jesus have mercy on me! Jesus have mercy on me! Jesus have mercy on me! Jesus have mercy on me! Jesus have mercy on me! Jesus have mercy on me!

Jesus have mercy on me! Jesus have mercy on me! Jesus have mercy on me! Jesus have mercy on me!

Jesus have mercy on me! Jesus have mercy on me! Jesus have mercy on me! Jesus have mercy on me! Jesus have mercy on me! Jesus have mercy on me! Jesus have mercy on me! Jesus have mercy on me! Jesus have mercy on me! Jesus have mercy on me!

Jesus have mercy on me! Jesus have mercy on me! Jesus have mercy on me! Jesus have mercy on me!

October 7th

The true Prophet speaks but people only hear the words of the fleshly false prophet. The things of God do not please the flesh, but they are meant to quicken the spirit. We must learn to try the spirits to see if they are from God.

Truth comes from above. We must worship the Father in Spirit and in Truth which is our reasonable service. We must learn to discern good from evil. Right from wrong. Truth from fiction.

Oh God, help us this morning to travel the right path. Help us to stay on that straight narrow path without wavering.

Oh Lord, we beseech thee with our whole heart. oh Lord Jesus, have mercy on us. Hear our cry this morning and deliver us from all our iniquities.

We pray that the true Prophet will always speak to us Your exact Word.

October 8th

The Peace of God is on me and with me this morning. The Joy of the Lord is my strength. I glory in all this, and my inner man rejoices.

What a Mighty God we serve. Our God is Awesome. There are no words in the English language that can totally describe how magnificent our Heavenly Father really is.

We live move and have our being. Our hearts are steadfast and focused. We give you all the praise, honor, and glory. We are seated in Heavenly places with Christ Jesus.

We will rejoice and be glad today. We will have a celebration with all the Heavenly Hosts and magnify Your Holy Name.

Draw us nearer. Nearer precious Lord. Nearer to Your Glory. Nearer to your Power. You are Holy.

Thank you, Jesus. Oh, Thank You Wonderful Jesus. Holy Spirit have Your way in our lives today!

God dwells in the spirit, self dwells in the soul, senses dwell in the body The soul is the meeting place of the spirit and the body. Your spirit has relationship with the spiritual world and Spirit of God. Your body is in contact with the world both affecting and being affected by it. Your soul stands between spirit and body yet belongs to both. It is linked with the spiritual world by the spirit and the material world through the body. Since your soul has the power of free will, it is able to choose which world it will live in.

Thus, your soul is composed of your mind, your will, and your emotions. Your spirit consists of, conscience, intuition, and fellowship. You decide which controls your body. Either you are a soulical being you flow with the dictates of this world or a spiritual being and led by Heaven.

Human beings were not created by God to be robots, but God has given us 'free will' to choose to follow His plan or follow satan's schemes. It's your choice? Choose who you are going to follow today?

The Chinese man's secret was found in a lock of hair that miraculously survived all those years as the body decomposed and that secret was about to lead our detectives to who was responsible for the old man's death.

I DIE BECAUSE OF MY BELIEF IN CHRIST. Was written on papyrus and was the only part of the original message that remained still readable from the lock of hair. Apparently, Li Wong Chang died because of his beliefs.

Our detectives had a possible motive, but the plot was about to thicken. Detective Ballew was about to touch on something.

While interviewing the Chang family he noticed a lot of Watchmen Nee reading material. When he inquired further, he found out that Chang was his wife's family name.

Was there a secret? That was about to be revealed. Was that old white haired Chinse man really Li Wong Chang?

A closer look at a picture in the living room was it a possible key? Skylark was familiar with the teachings of Watchman Nee and asked if he could make a copy and return it. The family were very cooperative and gave their permission.

The detectives' minds flashed back to thirty years ago. When the four of them were walking from the pizza shop and as they walked past, The Golden Dragon, they heard several men speaking or rather arguing in Chinese. The men wound up in the street wielding weapons. They ran to a nearby building where they ducked so they couldn't be seen. One of the Asian men struck what appeared to be an old white haired Chinese man with a green bladed sword. The old man fell to the ground and the other men quickly fled. They decided the coast was clear and ran over to investigate. When they got close enough to examine the sidewalk, the man's body instantly disappeared. How long had they remained hidden? What hadn't they seen? Think?

Chapter Ten

"TURN OFF YOUR BRAIN"

The name(s) of Brother Lawrence, Francois Fenelon, Madam Guyon, John Bunyan, Jonathan Edwards, John Wesley, Charles Wesley, George Mueller, George Whitefield, Hudson Taylor, Andrew Murray, A. B. Simpson, T. Austin Sparks, Praying Hyde, Charles Spurgeon, Charles Finney, Dwight L. Moody, Maria Woodworth-Etter, Jessie Penn-Lewis, William J. Seymour, John G. Lake, Mother Dabney are just a few of the mighty men and women of God that Holy Spirit used to bring revival all around the world.

As we learn to turn off our brains only then are we able to take in new information. We live in an age where technology rules and often turn off our brains and tune in to the god Siri and Alexa to name a few. We worship, iPhone, iPad and smartphone as our god. Who needs to go to the library for research when your have your laptop or desktop computer? We are being trained not to think but to react. In case you missed it you have already turned off your brain.

The passive mind is a battlefield constantly being attacked and lulled to sleep by enemy outside forces created to act like allies, but they are actually adversaries. Some of us don't even know our own personal phone numbers not to mention how to give directions. Your smartphone has replaced your brain.

The mind is lulled through 21st century lullabies such as alcohol, opium, cannabis, blue lotus, tobacco. Science and technology have improved the potency and, in some cases, have made them legal and easy to obtain. Mental illness and drug addiction has been sugar coated and given new more social friendly names, like social ills or it's the norm, like we all have these problems *"and if you can't be with the one you love, love the one you're with."*

Sebastian walked into a store and legally purchased an alcoholic beverage but when he opened it to drink it, he was immediately placed under arrest under the open container law which prohibits consumption of alcohol in public spaces. Yet Merv is allowed to use CBD which has concentration of THC freely and legally without the consequence of being arrested. The logic being that CBD doesn't qualify as a controlled substance and doesn't cause impairment. Neither does opening an alcoholic beverage but if enough is consumed or misused it can and may cause serious impairment. Either one can turn off your brain at any time.

Think About It

Does a clean house indicate that there is a broken computer in it?

Why is it that no matter what color of bubble bath you use the bubbles are always white?

Is there ever a day when mattresses are not on sale?

Why do people constantly return to the refrigerator with the hopes that something new to eat will have materialized?

Why do people keep running over a string a dozen times with their vacuum cleaner, then reach down, pick it up, examine it, then put it down to give their vacuum one more chance?

How do those dead bugs get into closed light fixtures?

Why do we wash bath towels? Aren't we clean when we use them? If not then what was the purpose of the bath?

Considering all the lint you get in your dryer, if you kept drying your clothes would they eventually just disappear?

When we are in the supermarket and someone rams our ankle with a shopping cart then apologizes for doing so, why do we say 'It's all right'? It isn't all right, so why don't we say, 'That hurt!'

Why is it that whenever you attempt to catch something that's falling off the table you always manage to knock something else over?

Is it true that the only difference between a yard sale and a trash pickup is how close to the road the stuff is placed?

First there is a mountain, then there is no mountain, then there is, what does that mean?

Why does a dog owner say their dog doesn't bite? All dogs bite!

HOW TO TURN OFF YOUR BRAIN AND LISTEN TO GOD

As I sit here in this darken place I want a way to get out
I know I need help so I start to scream and shout
I scream so loud with all the breath that I have in me
I scream so loud that I faint and fall to my knees
It is here I look up and see a bright but distant light
Then I hear a voice say I will help to make it right
So I start to climb the walls of this darken place
The closer I get to the light I start picking up the pace
My hand start to grow weary I fear that I might fall
When I hear that voice again saying let go of the wall
So I let go and find I am not falling but standing on the ground
But the light still draws closer it's almost all around
Even though I not moving the light stills draw near
I catch a glimpse of the darkness as it quickly disappears
As the light illuminates, I see how far I fell
I realize I was on the path that leads straight to hell
But now I see the right path and that is where I'll stay
Never forgetting the fear, I felt on the darken day
The fear of being alone with no one around
In the darken pit that was so deep underground
I still have fear but it is a fear of God that lives within me
My lord my Savior Jesus Christ has now set me free
I am so grateful he showed me that no matter how far I fall
To just let go and trust him and he'll be there through it all

The Maker of all human beings is recalling all units manufactured, regardless of make or year, due to a serious defect in the primary and central component of the heart. This is due to a malfunction in the original prototype units code named Adam and Eve, resulting in the reproduction of the same defect in all subsequent units. This defect has been placed in the '**S**top It **N**ow,' or the **SIN** Bin. The number to call for repair is **P-R-A-Y-E-R**.

Some other symptoms include:

1. Loss of direction
2. Foul vocal emissions
3. Lack of peace and joy
4. Selfish or violent behavior
5. Depression or confusion in the mental component
6. Idolatry
7. Rebellion

The Manufacturer, who is neither liable nor at fault for this defect, is providing factory-authorized repair and service free of charge to correct this SIN defect. The Repair Technician, Jesus, has most generously offered to bear the entire burden of the staggering cost of these repairs.

Once connected, please upload your burden of SIN through the REPENTANCE procedure. Next, download REMISSION from the Repair Technician, Jesus, into the heart component. No matter how big or small the SIN defect is, Jesus will replace it with:

1. Love
2. Joy
3. Peace
4. Patience
5. Kindness
6. Goodness
7. Faithfulness

8. Gentleness
9. Self-control

Please see the operating manual, the **B.I.B.L.E.** (**Basic Instructions Before Leaving Earth**), for further details on the use of these fixes.

WARNING: Continuing to operate the human being unit without correction voids any manufacturer warranties, exposing the unit to dangers and problems too numerous to list and will result in the human unit being permanently impounded.

DANGER: The human being units not responding to this recall action will need to be scrapped in the furnace. The SIN defect will not be permitted to enter Heaven so as to prevent contamination of that facility.

Thank you for your prompt attention. **GOD**

Brenda was almost halfway to the top of the tremendous granite cliff. She was standing on a ledge where she was taking a breather during this, her first rock climb. As she rested there, the safety rope snapped against her eye and knocked out her contact lens.

'Great', she thought. 'Here I am on a rock ledge, hundreds of feet from the bottom and hundreds of feet to the top of this cliff, and now my sight is blurry.'

She looked and looked, hoping that somehow it had landed on the ledge. But it just wasn't there.

She felt the panic rising in her, so she began praying. She prayed for calm, and she prayed that she may find her contact lens.

When she got to the top, a friend examined her eye and her clothing for the lens, but it was not to be found. Although she was calm now that she was at the top, she was saddened because she could not clearly see across the range of mountains.

She thought of the bible verse 'The eyes of the Lord run to and from throughout the whole earth.'

She thought, 'Lord, You can see all these mountains. You know every stone and leaf, and You know exactly where my contact lens is. Please help me.'

Later, when they had hiked down the trail to the bottom of the cliff, they met another party of climbers just starting up the face of the cliff.

One of them shouted out, 'Hey, you guys! Anybody lose a contact lens?'

Well, that would be startling enough, but you know why the climber saw it? An ant was moving slowly across a twig on the face of the rock, carrying it!

Lord, you can use anything in answer to prayer. Even a tiny ant. Remember there is nothing too hard for God. He never calls the qualified. He qualifies the called.

They all met back at the site where this story began (chapter 9) and tried to reenact what took place. They determined that they had remained hidden for a long time. What happened after the old Chinese man hit the ground? Exactly how long had they remained hidden? And why hadn't anybody in the Chinese Restaurant seen anything?

The detectives and their gumshoe wives decided to take a closer look at what remained of the Golden Dragon Restaurant, and they discovered something interesting. They found a small opening near the side of the building which led to a ramp and then a narrow flight of stairs. Why hadn't they seen this before?

The ten…nine and a half years olds had assumed blood because of the sword but all they really saw was the green sword being swung and the Chinese man fall to the ground.

Terrified and scared the children looked for a place to hide and huddled together for a short time before mustering up the courage to further investigate. By that time the old man had managed to disappear through that secret entrance and because the Golden Dragon had no windows no one saw what happened.

Now that they had pieced together that the Chinese man was able to escape from his attackers. They now needed to find out, who these attackers were and why did they target Li Wong Chang.

The detectives next enlisted the assistance of Sammo Chan a Chinese detective to determine if this was a random attack or the work or a Triad. Detective Chan was briefed on the case and visited the crime scene and made a most interesting discovery that the first investigative team overlooked.

Detective Chan informed the detectives that the body that was found could not have been Li Wong Chang. If not Chang, then who? The plot was about to thicken.

Sky and Ballew had to go back to the drawing board. That lock of hair contained the answer to the questions. Who was that man?

Does the Chang family know something that they are not telling us? The clue that was overlooked was a charred copy of Watchman Nee's book, *"The Spiritual Man"*.

There are three ways for believers to overcome death:

> *(1) by trusting we will not die until our work is finished.*
>
> *2) by having no fear of death even should it come.*
>
> *(3) by believing we will be delivered completely from death since we shall be raptured at the Lord's return. (Taken from The Spiritual Man – Watchman Nee)*

Detective Pacheco spied Skylark as he was getting ready to call it a day. *"Hey, lieutenant, Got a minute?"* *"Sure, detective"* he said as he walked over to her desk. *"You won't believe what happened today?"* *"Try me, Pacheco."* *"The squad invited me out tonight to Car 54's"* *"Well, it's about time you were appreciated around here, Ana."* *"Your actions today saved lives and I put you in for a commendation with the mayor, he's my close friend you know."* *"Thank you, L-T."*

"Lieutenant Skylark, there is a question I have been meaning to ask you?" *"Well, what are you waiting for detective?"* *"That black book you*

always carry with you...what's the name of it?" "Detective Pacheco, that little book is 'Sherlock Holmes and The Needle's Eye' and it has helped me to solve some of my most difficult cases. If you have some time, I'll share with you a quick story of how I came by this book."

"About 30 years ago, Detective Ballew and I were assigned to the case of a body that was found in a fire at the Golden Dragon Restaurant on Fifth and Ninth. The body, one of an old Chinese man contained no identification. The body was brought to the morgue and an autopsy was performed to determine cause of death and for identification. Ballew's wife Thik was working in the coroner office and performed the examination and determined that the cause of death was blunt force trauma."

"The case was assessed a homicide and handed over to us for investigation. We first needed to identify the victim, so we searched through the missing person files from thirty years ago. We arrived at 30 because as nine-and-a-half-year-olds, Ballew, myself, Thik and my wife Rod witnessed an old white-haired Chinese man being attacked by some men with a sword. But when we went to further investigate as kids, we couldn't find the old Chinese man."

"The name Li Wong Chang fit the description of the found remains and we contacted the family, and they confirmed our suspicions. We had a name, so we attached it to the body but now we needed a motive.

The only other clue we had was a fragment from a note found in a preserved lock of his white hair that read:

I DIE BECAUSE OF MY BELIEF IN CHRIST.

"Detective Chan an expert on Chinese affairs was enlisted to assist us and upon examination of the crime scene he discovered the remains of a charred book: 'The Spiritual Man' by Watchman Nee, he also determined that the body we found could not possibly be Li Wong Chang."

"Detective Ballew, Chan and I were leaving the cellar basement of the Golden Dragon where the body of the Chinese man was found, and I tripped and fell and as I was getting up, I spotted the black book that you always see me carrying."

"Lieutenant, this story is starting to get interesting, but can we continue tomorrow?" "Oh, I almost forgot, it's your acceptance to the team

night. Yes, come by my office around one and we'll do lunch at Rosalita's." Pacheco said, *"Date."* *as she logged off her computer and headed out the station.*

It was a calm clear cool night. Not a cloud in the sky and a full moon was slowly making its way into the picture. Suddenly out of nowhere a car came speeding down Third Street, mounted the sidewalk and came to a complete rest between Max's Florist and Mr. Kim's Dry Cleaners.

Detective Lieutenant Percival Timothy Skylark was about to leave the station when the call came in. He immediately ran the short distance to Third Street and saw a black Dodge Charger wedged between the two stores. He quickly noticed Detective Pacheco examining the wedged vehicle and shaking her head as she was visibly shaken. When she saw Lieutenant Skylark she walked straight into his arms, and he held her like he would his daughter who just survived a narrow escape.

"Lieutenant, if you hadn't stop to tell me your story, I might be lying underneath that vehicle." With tears rolling down her copper cheeks. "I never believed in divine intervention or God, but I do now." The two remained in that embrace as the Police, EMT's and Fire Department arrived on the scene. The driver was killed instantly and other than property damage to the two stores no one else was hurt. Lieutenant Skylark took Ana Pacheco home. The welcome to the squad party would have to wait for another time.

Ana took out her key and slowly opened her front door as Percival Timothy Skylark waited for her to walk safely inside. She closed the door behind her and threw her jacket on the couch. She went into the bathroom and prepared to take a soothing, relaxing bath with scented candles and essentials oils.

As she slowly undressed and slipped into the baptismal pool, she recited the sinner's prayer and slowly dipped her head under the water, when Ana Pacheco's head came up the Holy Spirit descended on her like a dove.

And I never felt this way before,

No never like this,
My life has changed.

I thought I had it all together,
Thought I was invincible,
Like a superhero – laugh.

But this feeling
I'm feeling now
Is out of this world.

Welcome to the Supernatural.........

Before his death, Watchman Nee left a piece of paper under his pillow which read: **"CHRIST IS THE SON OF GOD WHO DIED FOR THE REDEMPTION OF SINNERS AND RESURRECTED AFTER THREE DAYS. THIS IS THE GREATEST TRUTH IN THE UNIVERSE. I DIE BECAUSE OF MY BELIEF IN CHRIST. WATCHMAN NEE"**

Watchman Nee was recorded to have died on May 30th, 1972, and his body cremated on June 1st, 1972. His family was only allowed to see the ashes and were shown the paper containing his last words.

The power in these words and the fear of them being fulfilled could perhaps have been the reason that his remains were cremated rather then buried. Were his captors afraid that his last words would be fulfilled? There are people that profess no belief in God that read, understand, and fear His Word.

Skylark and Pacheco met at Rosalita's and ordered La Bandera (rice, red beans, meat, and salad). *"You're glowing, Pacheco!" "I know, I know, Lieutenant, 'nunca me senti major' (I have never felt better). 'Tengo a Jesus' (I have Jesus). Enough about me, are you going to finish the story?"*

"Where was I.........I tripped and fell, and I picked up the book. Funny, it wasn't charred and didn't smell like smoke. And I wondered, how did it get there? Then I looked at Chan and Ballew and said, "This don't add up." It was obvious that somebody else was here and recently *as I examined the condition of the book. It was fairly new and recent. It couldn't belong to the deceased. How did it get there?"*

"I went back to the station and began to read the book. And then it hit me as I read the Foreword, the clue to solving the case of the 'Chinese Man' lied in the scriptures. So, I immediately contacted Ballew and we opened our Bibles."

*"We turned off our brains and started a process that not only helped us to solve this case, but it became our: Basic **I**nstructions **B**enefiting **L**aw **E**nforcement for solving all our future cases."*

"Guau!" (wow) "You can say that again, Pacheco!" "And before I forget, here's your Bible, we have our Christian Law Enforcement Officers Meeting every Thursday at the community center at 7."

"Thanks, L-T. I'll be there!"

The waitress brought over their meal and the two detectives were so famished that they tore into their meal in silence. Lieutenant Detective Skylark would have to finish his story at another time.

Almighty God, Your Great Power and Eternal Wisdom Embraces the Universe, Watch Over All Policemen and Law Enforcement Officers. Protect Them from Harm in the Performance of Their Duty to Stop Crime, Robberies, Riots, and Violence. **O God and Heavenly Father**, Grant to them the serenity of mind to accept that which cannot be changed; courage to change that which can be changed, and wisdom to know the one from the other, through Jesus Christ our Lord, Amen.

CHRIST IS THE SON OF GOD WHO DIED FOR THE REDEMPTION OF SINNERS AND RESURRECTED AFTER THREE DAYS. THIS IS THE GREATEST TRUTH IN THE UNIVERSE.

Without this important doctrine in The Bible, we have no basis for what we call Christianity. History testifies that Jesus was born and died via crucifixion. But the debate will always lie in the fact of His Resurrection.

Did Jesus actually rise from the dead?

The four gospels in the New Testament of the Holy Bible documented by four different writers as well as many eye witnesses testify to the fact that Jesus indeed died for the redemption of sinners and resurrected in three days and was not only seen but examined by eleven of his chosen disciples.

The Book of Acts (Holy Bible) speaks of the Resurrected Jesus being seen for forty days before being taken up in Heaven and that my friends is the greatest truth in the universe.

So, what I am asking you to do right now is, turn off your brain. Turn off your brain to:

- Godlessness
- Sexual immorality
- Fear
- Envy
- Jealousy
- Hatred
- Sickness
- Addictions
- Quarreling
- Murder
- Selfishness
- Stress
- Ego
- Pain
- Suffering

I am asking you as chapter ten, comes to a close, if you get nothing else out of this book, get this:

Science, Technology, Philosophy, Modernity
and even New Age or any other Religion will not teach you,

'THE GREATEST TRUTH IN THE UNIVERSE'.

A truth we are reminded of each time we look at our calendar or at our clock,

'CHRIST IS THE SON OF GOD WHO DIED
FOR THE REDEMPTION OF SINNERS
AND RESURRECTED AFTER THREE DAYS.'
THIS IS THE GREATEST TRUTH IN THE UNIVERSE.'

CONCLUSION

I hope you had as much fun reading this book as I had hearing from God. The first time I learned how to turn off my brain I was in a dark place. I was drifting in a sea of loneliness and despair. I was being tormented and tortured by the worst kinds of demons. Then I heard and saw a soothing iridescent voice calling out to me, asking me, imploring me to be still. My brain shut off instantly and I experienced the Living God for the first time.

I had no idea what was happened to me, but something was happening to me. All my fear and inhabitation left me when I was in what I later knew to be, 'the secret place.' My conscious thoughts on what was going on in the world, I wasn't cognizant of anything going on around me. I had such a feeling of perfect peace in my life. My soul caged and my spirit released joy unspeakable. You can only imagine what these encounters with the Creator of the Universe were like, but this was only the beginning.

I was being taught how to experience God's Presence not just in the privacy of my home but also, I was being transformed as my mind was being renewed, suddenly I could sense and feel His Presence everywhere I went and in everything I did. My steps and movements were being ordered and guided by God Almighty.

Then one day, I heard God say: **"LISTEN"** and a priceless relationship began that is more valuable to me than anything money can buy. I had learned to **"Turn Off My Brain and Listen To God!"**

And you can too……..I know, you are like me and you want to believe in something. *"Tommy, can you hear me?"* People will always disappoint you; marriage can end in divorce. Jobs end. Relationships end. Friendships end. You end. But God never ends.

Can you all agree with me? Let's start a movement! Let's turn off the TV. Turn off our smartphones. Turn off our laptops and PC'S. Turn off the freeway and turn off our brains and listen to God.

Purpose with me to make yourself and the world a better place. What have you got to lose?

TURN OFF YOUR BRAIN AND LISTEN TO GOD

ABOUT THE AUTHOR

Tarrent-Arthur Henry writes under the name Tarrent-'Authur' Henry is a husband and step-father of two wonderful young men, He is the founder and guiding force of 'Righteous Uplifting Nourishing International, Inc'. a 501c3 Non-Profit Organization whose global mission is to empower people by showing them how to live their dreams. The Co-host of 'Transforming Lives' which is hosted by his wife, Helen Cummings-Henry. He is a Writer, Author, Poet, Pastor, Chaplain, Disaster Relief and Mental Health Specialist and a Certified Coach, Speaker, Teacher, and Trainer with Maxwell Leadership. The quote he lives his life by is: "Helping one person may not change the world but it can change the world for one person."

To Contact the Author:

Email Address:
info@authurhenry.com

Website:
www.authurhenry.com
www.intlrun.org

www.ingramcontent.com/pod-product-compliance
Lightning Source LLC
Chambersburg PA
CBHW071855070526
44583CB00016B/1697